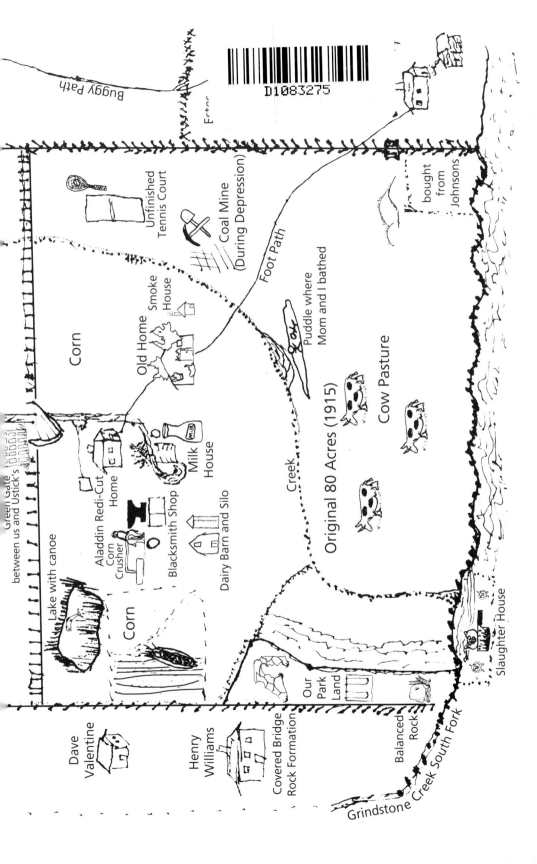

Buggy Path

D1083275

Unfinished Tennis Court

Coal Mine (During Depression)

Foot Path

bought from Johnsons

Smoke House

Old Home

Corn

Puddle where Mom and I bathed

Milk House

Aladdin Redi-Cut Corn Home Crusher

Blacksmith Shop

Dairy Barn and Silo

Creek

Original 80 Acres (1915)

Cow Pasture

Green Gate between us and Ustick's

Lake with canoe

Corn

Our Park Land

Slaughter House

Dave Valentine

Henry Williams

Covered Bridge Rock Formation

Balanced Rock

Grindstone Creek South Fork

GRANNY'S NOTES

GRANNY'S NOTES
"My First 84 Years"

BY SUE GERARD

To one of my Bryan Relatives — Hope you get a lot more information to share —

Sue Gerard

a **whip-poor-will** book

FRONT COVER PHOTO: "MY FIRST SWIMSUIT"

I sold Christmas trees, gooseberries and black walnuts to amass a fortune of about $30 by age 10. From this I wrote a $5 check for a bright red, all wool swimsuit because I was going to the new public swimming pool at the south end of College Avenue in Columbia. They had this wonderful slide and I loved flying down and splashing into the water. I'd go right back up the ladder to do it again. And again. What a great afternoon I had!

In the dressing room, however, I discovered that the seat of my new red swimsuit was worn threadbare!

Sue Gerard

Contributing Artists:
Cole Gerard
Oliver Gerard
Peter Gerard
Chris Graham
Sam Russell

Staff

Jacket Design:
Peter Gerard

Nancy Russell:	Managing Editor
Peter Gerard:	Designer/Producer
Cheryl Riley:	Copy Editor

Published by
Whip-Poor-Will Books
2000 E. Broadway #277
Columbia, MO 65201
http://grannys.home.ml.org/
grannysnotes@usa.net

Library of Congress Catalog Card Number: 98-96726
International Standard Book Number: 0-9667550-0-6

Printed in the United States of America
First Edition: November 1998

Dedicated to
W.F. "Chub" Gerard

1910-1998

CONTENTS

THANK YOU!

... to Hank Waters and Jim Robertson who have edited and published "Granny's Notes" in The Columbia Daily Tribune for the last 200 Tuesdays.

... to all of you who said, "You don't know me but I read your stories every week and you should write a book." You know who you are, including writer Joan Gilbert who made that suggestion 30 years ago.

... to family and friends who guided the project through, especially Designer and Producer Peter Gerard; Editor Cheryl Riley; and Managing Editor Nancy Russell.

... to Business Manager Walt Johnson-Gerard and assistants: Jennifer Graham, Mary Johnson-Gerard and Mike Russell.

... to artists: Cole Gerard, Oliver Gerard, Christopher Graham, Tim Graham, Sam Russell and Charlotte Stradford.

... to photographers: Linda Bryant, Lewis Garrotto, Janice "Cookie" Hagan, William Helvey, James Meyers, John Middleton, Cheryl Riley and those who could not be identified.

INTRODUCTION

One day a woman handed me convincing literature on "Raising Giant Bullfrogs for fun and profit." She knew that earning money was one of the motivations in my busy, happy life. Hooking a bullfrog on a plastic worm is the kind of competition I love. I enjoy winning a swimming race, a fiddle contest, a liar's contest or a game of rummy.

The joy of doing the impossible surfaced before I was old enough to remember and it sent Mom into hysterics because of a climb I made at age three.

Dad's dairy customers launched me into business by buying gooseberries, Christmas trees and black walnuts. I made 75 cents a day for punching wires though the worn out blocks in an old hay baler and I won a pocket full of dimes gambling at a festival. Mom and I loved going to the woods to bring back leaf mold for her flower beds. We often stripped off and bathed in a knee-deep water hole in the creek.

Competition kept me pedaling all day in rain on my bike and I felt that I'd accomplished the impossible when my front wheel crossed the hundred mile mark. (Later I repeated that feat seven more times!)

My kids and I stayed up all night to seine five wiggly grunion on a California beach. When I was 17, a locomotive engineer handed me his gloves and said, "This is the throttle and this toots the whistle. Have at it." So I drove Wabash Engine Number 2433 for seven miles.

After teaching water sports and recreation for 33 years at Christian (now Columbia) College, I taught myself to dig and prepare clay for little sculptures which tell "History in Three Dimensions." Then I bought a potter's wheel and a wood-burning, salt-glazing kiln. I'm hoping to fire it for the 21st time next spring.

Thinking it over, maybe I *should* try raising bullfrogs for fun and profit. When I get old?

A VERY LONG TIME AGO

Mom wrote, "I discovered Sue, with a line in each hand, shaking them and hollering, 'Whoa Boat,'" before my second birthday.

46 MILES BY BUGGY
PAID OFF

People along the country roads between Bellflower and Moscow Mills, Missouri, could set their clocks by the passing of O. D. Meyers and his horse and buggy. The well-dressed farmer drove east on Friday afternoons and back west late on Sundays. He stayed with his sister Mamie and her family in 1911 because he was courting Nancy Henry. Dad was farming with his father, and Nancy's parents owned the general store and saddlery in Moscow. Late on Sundays he'd head back home to Bellflower and let the horse go it alone while he slept. Sometimes he woke at daylight on Mondays with the horse standing at his barnyard gate.

Nancy was an accomplished musician who lived most of her life in the Centralia area and was in love with a poor farmer. They married in February, 1912; by the next February they were expecting a baby. This posed a problem because flood waters had destroyed their first crop. Then came an opportunity to go into partnership with Nancy's brother in the dairy business at Columbia. They milked by hand, cooled the milk overnight and then loaded cans into a box-shaped, four-wheel cart and drove the horse from house to house of their customers.

O. D. would go to the back door and shout "Milk." The woman would bring some kind of vessel to hold the milk. He used a tall metal measuring cup marked off for one, two, three or four quarts. O. D. and Nancy worked hard and prospered.

Drawing by Cole Gerard

ABOUT PEOPLE AND PLACES, WAY BACK

They stuck together, those pioneers who pushed the frontier into Kentucky. Survival in the 1700s depended on marksmanship, woodsmanship and friendship with each other—and with the natives. They protected themselves by constructing cabins near each other and by making an enclosure or stockade by driving long stakes into the ground, close together. When the going got rough families with weaker defenses closed their forts and were taken into stronger ones. Three of these forts, located near each other, were Boonesborough, Bryan's Station and Logan's Fort. These people followed the leadership of Daniel, the Boone with the itchy feet.

Boone's wife, the former Rebecca Bryan, was new to the wilderness as were her Tory parents. The third family name in this group was Logan. Their log homes and stockades were known as Boonesborough, Bryan's Station and Logan's Fort. Daniel and his sons made salt at Blue Licks in that area, as salt was important in curing pelts and preserving meat.

At the turn of the century when Daniel and Becky Boone moved to "Upper Louisiana," now called Missouri, most of the others came along. Over the years there were several marriages linking the Bryan, Boone and Logan families and many of us who are their descendants still live in Mid Missouri. My mother was a fifth-generation niece of Rebecca Bryan Boone and was also related to Corelia Logan Bryan.

Young (Daniel) Morgan Boone had bought land and built a cabin west of St. Louis and he urged his father to do the same. "But I'm 65 years old," Daniel Boone said. "That's a mite too old to pull up stakes and move again." Then 16 year-old Nathan mentioned "elbow room" and the troubles with Kentucky's land officials.

That did it! Most of the Bryans and Logans and many others came with the old explorer and his family and settled in St. Charles County. They set off in September, 1799, with the men driving the livestock overland, Morgan and Nathan accompanying most of the women and children in dug out canoes, arriving just after 1800.

My arrival in Missouri was 114 years later! 🐄

COWARDS DIDN'T LEAVE HOME IN COVERED WAGONS

Daniel Boone probably didn't consult his wife Rebecca about moving. Nathan, their 18-year-old son, urged his dad to move to Missouri, but when he kissed Olive Van Bibber, his sweetheart, goodbye, he knew he should have married her. About 75 miles down the river, he left Morgan with the canoes and headed back on foot, buying a marriage license on the way.

They married and packed for the long overland trip to Missouri. A few days later they rode off on two ponies and led a pack horse. They cooked over an open fire and slept on the ground. Olive wrote a diary of the 800-mile trip, admitting that "it was quite an undertaking for a couple so young."

Their destination was La Charette west of St. Louis. When they reached St. Louis, someone offered to trade Nathan 80 acres of land in downtown St. Louis for one of his ponies. He refused, saying he wouldn't trade that pony for the whole city of St. Louis.

Arriving earlier, Daniel and Becky (Rebecca Bryan Boone, my ancestor) built a dirt floor log cabin with the usual small windows, low door and fireplace. They never lived in a home that had a floor! They did, however, help Nathan and Olive plan and build a beautiful, limestone mansion, begun in 1803 and completed seven years later.

The whole of central Missouri became known as Boone's Lick Country and the trail across from Nathan's home in St. Charles County to the salt licks in Howard County was called Boone's Lick Trail. The early route took the ox teams and wagons six miles north of Columbia, but the route was shifted to the south in 1823 so travelers could get supplies in Columbia. A scar in the earth east of Columbia near Highway WW is identified in the abstract as the old road which "crosses the North Fork of Grindstone Creek—150 yards downstream from an outcropping of coal on the Allen Park place." That's behind Mike and Nancy's home and Friends Together Antiques.

Wagons entering Columbia about two miles from this spot were faced with climbing a muddy hill on what the 1876 Atlas of Boone County called "Spring Street." When word reached downtown Columbia that wagons were approaching on the trail, men hitched up their mule teams and went out to help, knowing that a big spring kept the hill muddy much of the time. The folks traveling in those wagons must have been greatly relieved to see the men coming with two-mule teams, chains and double trees to help get them moving again.

As overland travelers often said, "Only lunatics attempted these trips. Cowards never left home!"

ONE HORSE AND A BOX WITH FOUR WHEELS

The retail dairy business has changed a lot since Dad began milking cows by hand and delivering the milk to customers' homes in a one-horse, box-type covered wagon. Mom was the bookkeeper. That was in 1912 and he was in partnership with his brother-in-law John L. Henry, an official in Boone County government. The dairy farm and the couple's home were adjacent to the present location of the Stephens College golf course. The cows likely grazed on that golf course land.

Dad, a frugal man of German stock, was soon able to buy his partner's half interest in the cows and equipment. In 1916 he and Mom moved, with two babies, to the 80 acres they bought four miles east of downtown Columbia, and a half mile south of Fulton Gravel Road. Their half-mile private driveway extended through another fellow's sheep pasture. Dad and his hired men filled the mud holes, and finally covered the whole half mile, using creek gravel, shovels and a gravel wagon pulled by two horses.

With more land, Dad was able to increase the size of his herd. He used good Holstein bulls and saved the heifer calves, year after year, to improve and enlarge his herd. He employed two sons of Henry and Annie Williams, neighboring landowners, to help with the farm and dairy work.

Dad built a hollow tile milk house and bought an old steam boiler to heat water for washing milk cans, buckets and, later, glass bottles. Soon he contracted for a 34-foot tall, Dickey hollow tile silo, made in St. Louis, for storing chopped corn to feed the cows. (I treasure my one silo tile which was rescued when the farm became El Chapparal subdivision.)

The cows lined up at the barn door waiting to get in to eat their mixture of silage, wheat bran, bright yellow cotton seed meal and a dash of salt. Each cow had her own stanchion and her own serving of food. Dad insisted on doing the feeding because he knew which cows would waste food if served too much and which ones were greedy. He'd put the neighboring cows' food out of reach of the greedy ones and he served larger helpings to Hoke, Charlotte and the other higher producers.

The cows ate as the men wiped their bags with damp cloths which smelled of disinfecting fluid. The men sat on one-legged stools and held the metal buckets between their knees as they squeezed the teats alternately – right hand, left hand, over and over. The white streams of milk flew into the bucket making a "squirk," "squirk" sound which changed as the cows gave their milk freely and the buckets filled. If the cow shifted her feet, the one-legged stool allowed the milker to rock back, out of the way, without getting to his feet.

At the evening milking time, several cats and kittens and I all went to the old gray wooden barn to get fresh warm milk. One man poured milk into a flat pan for the cats and kittens. One of the fellows would squirt milk, directly from the cow, into my bottle. I didn't like the foam so I waited until it settled and then drank the milk as I walked the path back to the house.

Dad planned to tear down the old barn in the summer of 1922 and build a new one before cold weather. He'd leave the feed bunks and stanchions in place and milk the cows under the open sky. When our house burned to the ground in May, however, all money, credit and energy went into building a new home and outfitting our family of four with clothing and the necessary furniture and accessories. Dad's new barn had to wait.

Cart and trucks, 1915-1938.

Jim and me at ages four and two.

BIRTH OF A TOMBOY

Mom was not thrilled to learn that she was pregnant again so soon. Her baby boy was learning to crawl and by late summer she'd have two babies in diapers! When Dr. Kampschmith came to deliver the second baby that hot July day, he went directly to the northwest bedroom where he had delivered Jim 16 months before. Soon he held the second baby by its feet, spanked it to make it yell, and said, "Nancy, this one's a girl."

Nancy Henry Meyers imagined a dainty little girl in a pink smocked organdy dress with ruffles. What she got, instead, was a tomboy who would beg to wear bib overalls to church. I was that tomboy. They named me Sue, just S-u-e. Dad had a sister Susie and Mom had a sister Susan. Searching for a middle name, Dad and Mom coined the name "Emelyn" honoring three creative, courageous women named Emeline.

Grandma Henry's bible had an insert relating that one of those Emelines carried a three-week-old infant in her arms on the trip from Kentucky to Missouri—800 miles on horseback! One was a weaver of wool coverlets. She required payment in silver and from those coins she hammered out coin silver spoons.

The Emeline I knew and loved was Mom's sister whom we called Aunt "Yine." She painted in water color and oil and did a bit of sculpture in various materials. I'm proud of those pioneers for whom I was named.

Dad and Mom's families were quite different. Dad's ancestors were poor, hard working farm people of German descent. His mother died at the time of Dad's brother Jess's birth and they were raised by their four half sisters. My favorite memories of Mom and Dad are of their happiness together. Dad whistled as he worked. Mom stopped her work, dried her hands on her apron and played the piano several times a day. They were very much in love. When Dad came in the back door, he'd pass through the kitchen and greet Mom with a love pat on her rump. Smiling, she'd pretend to hit him.

Mom, with poor vision, was an accomplished pianist, but was shielded from sports lest she break her glasses! She never discussed the fact that she was deathly afraid of water. She loved the out-of-doors and being in the woods and she taught Jim and me to like animals and gardening. She realized, early on, that she and I would be great companions for the rest of her life.

DAD'S MULE RIDE

When Dad and Mom moved to Boone County after their marriage in 1912, they left Lincoln County with little money. A flood had destroyed their first corn crop and Mom was pregnant. They went into partnership on a dairy with Uncle John Henry. About three years later they were able to purchase their own eighty acre dairy farm.

I've never known how they moved the furniture and other belongings, but the old mule came from Lincoln on foot. Dad went back to Bellflower and bought a mule. He bridled, mounted and started a long, hard day's ride to Columbia. Somewhere along the way, he spotted something lying in the road. When he picked it up, he found it was a leather-bound Rand McNally road map of the United States. He got back on the mule and as he continued his journey, he thumbed through the oilskin pages of that atlas. He found it a great relief from the boredom of his ride and boned up on his eighth grade geography. He dreamed of seeing California and the Grand Canyon some day. He followed the route he was on from Bellflower to Columbia. He located San Diego where his brother, Uncle Jess, made stacks of money as a card dealer in the casinos of Tia Juana, Mexico, just across the border.

As he traveled on the mule and also in his mind, a car pulled up beside him and stopped. "Whoa!" Dad stopped the mule and the stranger said, "Hey, fella. How do you get to Calwood?"

"I can't rightly say because I'm a stranger here myself," Dad must have answered. Then he remembered the map in his hand. "But I can look it up."

Imagine the puzzlement of that traveler when Dad unsnapped the leather binding of his folded Rand McNally Atlas of the United States, thumbed through the pages to find Missouri, hunted the route and finally came up with the directions to Calwood, all while sitting on the back of a slow-walking, old Missouri mule!

That leather-bound volume would be worth a pretty penny today, but sadly Dad's map burned when we lost everything in the fire that destroyed our home in 1922.

"But I'll never forget the look on that man's face," Dad told me, "as he gunned the car's engine and sped off!"

SMITHTON LASTED ONLY THREE YEARS

The first settlement in this area was a cluster of about five hastily built log cabins and Richard Gentry's store and tavern. A U.S. Government Land office opened at Franklin in 1818, west of here, offering fertile land for four dollars to six dollars per acre. The land agent there was named Thomas A. Smith. Landowners named their fledgling town for this nice man. "Smithton" it was, but it lasted only three years.

Smithton, like Franklin, was doomed. Smithton had too little water and Franklin had too much! By 1828, only 10 years after the land office was opened, Franklin was suddenly washed away by the treacherous Missouri River. It had grown to include a newspaper, two academies of learning, a public library, a jail, three taverns, five stores, a tobacco factory, six Baptist Churches and more! Suddenly Franklin was gone.

Smithton was situated on the hill west of present-day downtown Columbia, approximately where the water tower's morning shadow touches the ground in the vicinity of Garth and Walnut. The search for a source of "living water" included the digging of a very deep hole into the earth. Having failed in their first attempt, they dug deeper – 60 feet – in a different location. Still no luck! A third hole was 90 feet down but didn't produce enough water!

In his History of Boone County, Edwin W. Stephens explained that it was unfortunate that people had not yet discovered that water could be collected in underground cisterns. There was endless water from a spring down the hill, but carrying water up that hill in buckets was torture! Smithton's cabins were dismantled and rebuilt down the hill where water was readily available.

What was life like in Smithton when it was one of the westernmost settlements? The cabins had only dirt floors; women made bed covers and rugs out of worn out clothing. In winter those rugs were hung over the small window holes as there was no glass. People went barefooted much of the time and homes had a library of one book – the Bible. Wagons traveled along the Boone's Lick Trail in a steady stream.

An outdoor toilet or "John" was a luxury in the wilderness because "behind a tree" was sufficient. Rain water from the roof was caught in a wooden barrel where birds and flies polluted it; "wiggle tails" swam there when flies' eggs hatched. Salt was needed for tanning hides, pickling cabbage for kraut, curing meat – and for food. Hunters traded skins for salt at the salt works where Daniel Boone's sons boiled water from a salt spring. That was good hunting ground too, because animals went there to lick the brackish earth where salt had been deposited for centuries.

Men located bee trees in the woods and cut them to harvest the honey. Blackberries, gooseberries, mushrooms and various kinds of nuts were gathered from the woods. People were dependent on each other and were ready to help when needed. The carpenter, tinner, blacksmith and leather craftsmen were important because the nearest store was about 25 miles away.

Many of the people who settled in this area were from Kentucky. Historians refer to them as responsible, enterprising, intelligent and thrifty. Many of their descendants are still here, linking us to 176 years of rugged history.

Grandpa Henry, on the right, was a farmer, a miller, a Confederate soldier and a merchant. This was his general store and saddlery.

THE LIFE OF A CONFEDERATE SOLDIER

Civil War soldiers didn't talk much about their experiences and there was little in our family Bible except names and dates. There was a note saying that my grandfather and one of his twin brothers fought in opposing armies and that they met in midstream during a lull in the fighting at Vicksburg. James Lawrence Henry, Jr. lived to be an old man who wore his derby hat in the house to keep his head warm.

In 1861 he enlisted in the Confederate Army. Even though he was wounded twice during the war, at its end, he walked home. It took him almost three months.

His first wife died leaving him with three children. He then married a young woman named Huldah Pratt, my grandmother. Hulda always called him "Mr. Henry," but I called him "Grampa." Huldah described the old soldier's later years in a letter she wrote in 1918.

Dear Brother Albert:

This morning your brother said, "This is Albert's 77th birthday," and I resolved to write today... Mr. Henry moves about home without the use of crutch or cane. He eats heartily, reads many books and papers, plays solitaire and plays cards after supper with our daughter Emeline, except on Sundays. Mr. Henry and I sing many good old hymns at twilight, after it's too dark to read or work... You may remember that "singing" was the key note that started our acquaintance. We have done lots of singing together in 33 years. Our marriage may have seemed to our friends as a "leap in the dark," but as far as I am concerned I could not have asked it to have been better...

Nancy has a good man, a bright son and a very sweet little Sue, named for her two aunts. Boy named Jim. They frequently come up in a car from Columbia and take us there to visit them... Mr. Henry can't get on a train. He has enjoyed many nice wheelchair rides. Many nice things are said about your kindness in sending it.

H.H.

The Missouri Historical Society's library contains James Lawrence Henry's response to a survey made in 1920 by the United Daughters of the Confederacy (UDC). He fought in 13 major battles: Baker's Creek, Big Black, Vicksburg, Kingston, Dalton, Newhope, Smyrna, Fire Mountain, Kenesaw Mt., Peachtree Creek, Atlanta, Altoona and Mobile.

Asked to relate "some impressive incident," Grampa wrote:

I was a prisoner in the Old Capitol, Wash., D.C. in the winter of 1862 when one morning about 150 of us were notified to be ready to go on exchange. As we were marching down to the landing on the Potomac, someone started singing "The Bonny Blue Flag" and every man joined in. The guards tried to stop it, threatening the bayonet, but it was no use...

Capt. H.C. McKinney of Boone County organized a temporary company to hold us together until we got over the Mississippi River and could rejoin our old commands. I had been elected Orderly Sergeant of Capt. Amos Hulett's Company.

When we reached Mississippi, Grant's campaign against Vicksburg was on and we volunteered to join Bowen's 1st Missouri Brigade, ... and were assigned to the 5th Regiment... The first real battle was Baker's Creek...

Captain McKinney was killed and our loss was 35 killed, wounded or missing. Our army fell back to Big Black River where we were routed, ... then we fell back into Vicksburg where we held the fort for 48 days, living on one fourth rations and, at the last, on mule meat and cowpea bread.

Then Grampa fired one last shot at the enemy as he wrote:

One thing I would like to impress on the minds of the United Daughters of Confederation: at the surrender of Vicksburg, no Yankee crossed our lines of entrenchments until we had marched outside of them and stacked our arms. We were starved out, not conquered...

I'm sorry I could not write this better and have had something more interesting to relate, but am nervous and old and have wheels in my head that don't mesh right. I am very truly yours, (signed) J.L. Henry

Grampa lived four more years and is buried beside Grandma in the Centralia cemetery.

Nancy Henry Meyers and Orlando Denver Meyers, Mom and Dad.

EYEGLASSES CHANGED MOM'S LIFE

When I was a kid, Mom used to get us out of bed on a stormy night and have us put on our shoes. After I was 10 years old I wore glasses and she made sure I had them on as well. Sometime in her youth there had been a "cyclone" in the Centralia area where she lived, and after the funnel passed, many people went out to see the damage. She never forgot that those who were forced out of bed in the night had cut their feet on broken glass, jagged lumber, exposed nails and other debris.

Mom often told me about how difficult it was to get glasses before 1900, and she saw to it that I was careful not to get mine broken. Centralia was 20 miles north of Columbia where the nearest "eye man," Dr. Betz, had his office.

"It took a long time to get glasses or repairs," she said. "Mama would write a letter to Dr. Betz and he'd write back, making an appointment."

Then Grandma and Mom would take the Wabash train from Centralia to Columbia on the day of the appointment. "Dr. Betz would take my glasses, recheck my eyes and make some notes. Then he'd send my glasses to St. Louis for the service."

The package would be mailed and carried on the Wabash train. The local spur to Columbia made a transfer in Centralia and would then be forwarded to St. Louis. After the St. Louis "eye man" ground the lens or whatever was to be done, he shipped the package back to Dr. Betz via Centralia and the local Columbia "spur." Dr. Betz then wrote to Grandma Henry and said that Little Nancy's glasses had arrived and that he would expect them on a certain day. He'd coordinate the appointment with the train schedule so Mom and her Mama could return home on the same day.

Wearing glasses in those days changed a person's life. Mom was not allowed to take chances with such things as baseball, basketball, volleyball and other sports. Instead she studied music, did intricate embroidery and became an excellent cook. When they were young women, Mom and Aunt Emeline took a class in professional candy making. They learned to make fondant, to dip chocolates and decorate candy. They sold fancy candies when they lived in Moscow Mills, Missouri, where Grandpa owned a "General Store and Saddlery."

After marrying Dad and having two children, she was a dairy farmer's wife and loved gardening, berry picking, hiking in the woods and lots of other outdoor activities. Mom and the milk customers became telephone friends and two or three of them liked to come out to spend the day. Sometimes they'd take skillet, lard, corn meal and garden vegetables to the woods and spend the day. They'd have their fishing poles and worms and were almost certain to catch creek perch and mud cats in the deep holes in Grindstone Creek.

Even with eyeglasses, Mom was still an outdoors person at heart.

"DEAR HOME FOLKS..."

In 1912, Nancy Bruton Henry, the daughter of a merchant, married Orlando Denver Meyers, a dairy farmer. They lived at the east edge of Columbia, Missouri, until they bought a farm four miles out of town. Grandma and Grandpa Henry feared that she'd be lonely so far out in the country, but her letter written in April, 1916, allayed their fears. Here is a condensed version of that letter:

Dear Home Folks:

No indeed, I won't get lonely here... Well, you ought to have seen the children when they found the rabbits. Words could not describe the antics they cut. Sue jumped up and down and climbed up in her chair and would have gone right over the table for them. Jim said, "Mother, can they bark?" Then they kissed and kissed them. Sue had to go back to their box and kiss them several times before she went to bed... Emeline, Sue is singing "Rosary" now.

I took the children down to the big rock and farther on, while Lando cut telephone poles. Found all kinds of ferns... Sue was more foolish about the water than Jim. She kept trying to get into it... The spring is brim full. It has living water in it.

Every minute I have I will be out of doors. Lando put in 6 acres of oats and timothy this week. I have 8 hens setting. Got 98 eggs yesterday, average over 7 dozen a day. Sold $8.55 worth in March despite the fact the hens were moved that month and stopped laying. I get 17 1/2 cents a dozen for them.

Papa talked about the children playing out when it gets warmer. They live out doors. Sue just yells when I take her sweater off. I have to keep an eye on them... The other day Gene (a student helper) harrowed the garden and left Steamboat hitched to the harrow. First thing we knew Sue was sitting on the board, hollering, "Whoa Boat" and shaking a line in each hand.

Jim writes 'T' for Tommie and 't' for kitten. He writes 'S' for Aunt Sue and 's' for his sister. Sue's new words: Night, spill, break, sorry, fall... She begs for "cocoa" which is sassafras tea. She was standing at the table in her little red chair and fell the other day. When Gene came in she met him at the door and said "fall." Then pointed at the table, chair and floor and said, "fell." Guess you are tiring of this foolishness so I will quit, anxiously awaiting a reply I am lovingly,

Nancy and family.

"SUE! SUE! SUE!"

Independent? Yes, fiercely so. I did what I wanted to do, whenever I wanted to do it, wherever I happened to be. First it was with the chickens' watering troughs, then the Mullen leaf cigars, then who knows what? Mom didn't know what to expect next, but she knew to expect surprises. The silo surprise sent her into hysterics.

She and Dad borrowed money to buy our 80-acre farm, several additional milk cows and a silo. Feed from a filled silo provided milk cows a substitute for grass during the winter months. Choosing a silo and seeing the huge loads of tiles arriving and being installed made exciting conversation in the family. Finally it was autumn and the corn was ripening, just the right stage for making ensilage. It took more than 20 men, six teams and wagons, and several women to help Mom on silo-filling day. I must have thought that I should learn, firsthand, about this important addition at the end of the barn.

When Mom went to feed the chickens, she spied something above the silo chute and discovered that I had climbed almost to the top of that 34-foot structure! She screamed, "Sue! Sue!

Sue!" and went into hysterics. Dad ran to her, grabbed her and held his hand over her mouth to quiet her. As a daring person himself, he said calmly, "Nancy! Don't yell. She got up there on her own. She'll get down safely—if you don't frighten her." He guessed right.

This picture shows the silo, on the right, with the newer barn and a wooden silo that was added later. Charlotte, the mother of twin calves, was such a heavy milk producer that the calves had to get down on the ground to suck. The photo shows the wooden enclosure, dark inside, which hides the ladder to the silo. I was above that when Mom became hysterical!

Of course I don't recall the incident. I was only <u>three years old</u>. 🐄

The calves had so much to drink they had to duck down to nurse. Mother screamed when she saw me above the silo's wooden chute.

DAD REALLY KNEW HOLSTEINS

Tall cylindrical towers called silos once dotted the countryside and when you saw a silo you could bet that dairy cows were grazing nearby. Producing and selling milk was hard work but a way for ambitious farmers to make a living. Silage, also called ensilage, was great feed for milk cows. It was made of chopped corn—stalk, ear, leaves and all—packed into airtight silos when the stalks were still partly green and the ear corn grains were matured but not dry.

There was enough moisture in the corn to mold if air reached it. In an airtight silo, however, it heated and fermented, creating a feed which cows craved. It took the place of green pasture grazing. They bawled when it was gone in the spring. Because cows liked it, they gave more milk eating silage than they did on dry feed. Silos were expensive and they had to be erected by professionals.

Mr. C. W. Furtney had loaned Dad and Mom money to buy their farm and other things. Dad explained to Furtney that the best feed produced the most milk and that the silo would pay for itself in time. With faith in the young couple's judgment, the man approved another loan. They selected a 34-foot tall, hollow tile silo made by The Dickey Tile Company in St. Louis. The tiles were salt-glazed ceramic squares which locked together to make the airtight cylinder, impervious inside and out.

That fall was the first of an annual event called silo filling day. Mom worked days ahead, preparing a big feed for about 30 people. Neighbor women helped serve the workmen at noon. It was a "trade work" arrangement where Dad helped neighbors thresh grain and Mom helped women feed the threshing crews. Kids had a great time together at all of the gatherings, but I was just three years old and do not remember these early events. That fall Dad climbed the ladder several times, reached down deep into the packed silage and brought up a sample to show Mom and let her smell its fragrance.

When it was ready to feed, he used a special wide pitchfork to toss the feed down the dark ladder chute to a big roller cart at barn floor level. He'd scatter it into the cows' feeding places and add bran, cottonseed meal and a sprinkling of salt for each animal. When he turned the cows in, each one went to her own special stanchion to eat the mixture that Dad fed according to each cow's diet needs. Dad was never too sick or too far from home to be there to do the feeding.

The stanchion was made of wood with a wooden block that locked the cow in place until released. It also kept the greedy ones from leaning far to one side and stealing a few bites with swipes of their long tongues.

The silo was at the south end of the old gray barn that Dad was hoping to replace. That plan changed, however, when our house burned in 1922.

Many people stood behind this hard-working young couple

and their little children.   Besides the farm and cows, Mr. Furtney and the bank helped with loans for a new home, new barn, dairy trucks, milking machines and even complete pasteurization and refrigerating systems. Dad had one of Columbia's leading dairies, serving Boone County Hospital from its beginning.   My parents proudly reached a longtime goal when Jim and I graduated from the University of Missouri in 1936 and had our own good jobs.

DYSART & HENRY, MILLERS

Boone County Plat Book for 1876 shows the location of a mill owned and operated by "Dysart and Henry," eight miles north of Columbia. According to Col. William F. Switzler's *History of Boone County*, their grinding mill could produce 35 barrels of flour or 300 bushels of corn meal per day. The building was 30' x 36' and was two and a half stories high.

Switzler continues: Messrs. Dysart and Henry could also "turn off 4,000 to 5,000 feet of hard lumber per day," and the mill was "the only one of its kind in the county except at Sturgeon."

Dysart and Henry used a 25-horsepower engine to drive the machinery, which was housed in an engine house measuring 17' x 46'. The machinery was called "the automatic grinding mill" and was from Logansport, Indiana. James L. Henry was Mother's father. He survived the Civil War and was a merchant and also operated a harness shop and saddlery. How I would have enjoyed watching those two men grind grain and saw wood! Thanks to Switzler, we know even this little bit about their enterprise.

MELON FEASTS
AT "FLAT ROCK"

Think back to the early 1920s. If you can't do that, just imagine that you are a little child living four miles from downtown Columbia during that time period. Your world included little more than neighbors, the dime store, the grocery store, church – and the Sears and Roebuck catalog. My early life was like that.

Our neighbors Mr. and Mrs. Sublett had seven children – six boys and Alie May, who was about my age. Their home faced Richland Road and their land backed up to the Fulton Gravel, which is now called Route WW. Bill Sublett was a truck farmer who raised fruit and vegetables to sell. His watermelons, cantaloupes and muskmelons grew in a sandy creek-bottom patch along the North Fork of Grindstone Creek. The patch was across the creek from rock formations that gave the water hole the name of Flat Rock.

In another garden, the Subletts raised potatoes, cabbage, beans, tomatoes, corn and other fruits and vegetables. They sold them in Columbia to hotels and restaurants in addition to their street "market." Farmers just chose a spot, parked and sold directly to consumers from their wagons. In those days the grocery stores didn't offer much in the way of perishable items, so this street market enterprise was popular with housewives. Some bought enough for canning and preserving. Freezers were unknown.

Depending on what was ripe, the older Sublett children and their parents would pick the vegetables early in the morning. They'd load sacks and baskets into a wagon and Bill would hitch up his horses and be in town before people went to work.

By the time he had secured the horses and set out water for them, the first customers were there with shopping bags and open pocketbooks. He often had produce, particularly melons, left at the end of the day and he shared these with friends and neighbors.

On hot summer evenings, more than a dozen men, women and children, plus several Subletts, would meet at Flat Rock for a cooling dip in the creek. I was too young to swim so I'd do what we called "the mud crawl." I did that with my feet splashing, my head up and my hands "walking" along on the sandy creek bottom. Most of us swam in the clothes we'd worn all day: men in bib overalls, kids in underwear or cutoff pants, women and older girls in dresses. Afterward, we'd pat our clothes dry with towels and go home wet.

People came and went, some on foot, some in buggies, a few in Model "T" Fords. Most people stayed until after dark and then lit their oil lanterns to light their way home.

Today, some people laugh at me because I like both salt and pepper on cantaloupe, muskmelons and watermelon. I learned to love that taste standing around Bill Sublett's melon wagon. We'd begin in the middle of a long slice of watermelon, eat the sweetest part to the ends, spit the seeds on the ground and wipe off the juice with our bare hands. Mr. and Mrs. Sublett cut slices as fast as our hands were empty or until our mothers made us stop. We tossed the rinds into a tub to be saved for the Sublett's chickens and pigs. He'd also save the seeds of a few very tasty melons, drying them and planting them the next year.

With friends like the Subletts and a water hole like Flat Rock, is it any wonder that I was grown before I heard the words "air conditioning?"

Billy with Jim and me. In the back-
ground is our house on the dairy farm
before it burned.

NANNY & BILLY

Farm kids' lives were not all work, of course. My brother was 16 months older and we didn't have many playmates except at church and community events. We made our own fun where we were, with what we had. I now know that this homemade recreation helped shape our lives.

Mom, a city girl, liked an excuse to go to the woods and she took us there before we were old enough to go alone. We gathered acorns and shiny, lopsided buckeyes and took them home to play with on rainy days. They became soldiers or hay bales or hen's eggs – treasures in our toy box. Dad carved acorns into little baskets or finger rings. I could hardly wait to have my own knife and even now I carry a tiny penknife and use it daily.

We had two goats, Nanny and Billy, that liked playing with Jim and me. They weren't milk goats, just plain white goats which we'd hitch to our wagon and pretend were horses. The hired men used to call me "Billy" and Gene Waters, an MU agriculture student who lived with us, called me "Nanny" for the rest of his life. Gene used to play marbles with Jim and me on the rug after supper, and he'd often let us ride about a half mile in his motorcycle side car on his way to school.

I got into trouble, before I was old enough to remember, for slopping around in the chicken's water with my shoes and stockings on. But I still like being in water. Jim and I didn't get in trouble for rolling up half-dry mullein leaves and trying to smoke them like cigars because nobody caught us. The taste was terrible and we couldn't make them burn anyway. So we tried to smoke coffee grounds and that tasted even worse. I'm sure this helped influence us to be nonsmokers.

Mom and I roamed in the woods, waded in shallow creeks, fished and often carried baskets of "leaf mold" back home for the flower beds. She helped me catch toads and woolly worms in my bare hands and we'd put them in a tub with rocks and grass and a jar lid of water, then release them later. I taught my four grandsons to do that too. They'd build a castle in moist sand and have toads and woolly worms for inhabitants. It was a victory when a worm crawled across the bridge over the moat and entered the castle door.

I was a tomboy and liked riding saplings in the woods. Hickory was best because it was flexible and strong and just the right size to bear my weight. I spent many happy hours in my favorite big maple tree in our backyard. Maybe that's where I learned the joy of leaving the world behind and being alone sometimes?

HAPPINESS WAS AN OLD MUSTY BARN

One of my fond memories is of dirty, smelly, old barns. I especially loved one that was partially falling down—a neighbor's log barn. In my mind's eye, I feel the dusty cobwebs on my face as I mentally climb the old pole ladder that was the stairway to the loft.

There sure was a lot to do in an old barn. There was soft-stacked hay for jumping on and rolling in. The greatest part of John Estes's barn was its loft. I'd climb the vertical ladder made out of sapling poles from the woods. Cobwebs, sagging from the weight of dust and chaff, would get in my face and hair as I climbed, but I couldn't let go of the ladder to brush them away lest I'd fall.

There were usually baby kittens in the loft and often a setting hen on a dozen or more eggs, feathers all ruffled up to cover them and keep them warm. Later, the same hen would be hovering chicks whose tiny heads stuck out from under her feathers. The old hen would cluck ominously to her babies saying, "You stay back under there or that kid will grab you and squeeze you to death." She'd peck me when I reached under her to get a chick. I learned to hold her head with one hand while I picked up a chick in the other. I'd cradle the chick in my hands and sing it to sleep as I did the kittens.

I always wondered how a hen ever got in that loft—certainly not by the vertical sapling ladder I had climbed! And I worried about the fact that there was no water in the loft for her. One day I saw her on the ground. She walked around, eying the loft's open door. Finally, when she was in the right spot, she ran, flapped her wings wildly and rose into the air still flapping. She just barely caught the loft boards and kept her balance. I worried no more.

One day I watched a black snake steal an egg from a loft nest. He spread his mouth wide and gradually stretched that tiny mouth enough to engulf the egg. His body bulged as the egg moved along. I guess the egg finally was digested, but the snake left before that happened.

Thinking about that old barn, I relive the good times and the exciting times I spent there as a child. The barn is gone, but surely I can find another barn. I must take my four little grandsons up a sapling pole ladder to a hay loft to look for kittens, baby chickens and maybe a snake stealing eggs. Saturday morning cartoons couldn't hold a candle to an experience like that!

DAD'S ICE HOUSE
WAS MY PLAY HOUSE

On a hot summer day, my favorite place to play was in the ice house, a large hole in the ground where Dad stored pond ice each winter. A ground-level, A-frame roof covered the hole and there was a narrow door in the gable end. This was where the ice went in during the winter and where it came out, as needed, during the summer. It was, of course, made of pond water and not used for human consumption. Instead, it was used to ice down glass bottles of milk to keep the milk from getting warm.

Dad would put a chunk of ice on top of each 12-quart crate and chip it up with an ice pick. He'd stack the crates into the Model T truck and cover them with a damp tarpaulin. He drove to town and then delivered milk to his customers by lifting the tarp and bringing out the chilled milk. His deliveries took him all over the town as he left bottles on customers' front porches or in their ice chests.

By July the remaining ice in the circular pit was well below ground level and I'd climb down a short wooden ladder to the "floor" of sawdust which covered the ice. My dolls and kittens and I considered it a fine play house on a hot summer day.

Today we'd say it had natural air conditioning.

It was a cold winter job putting up ice from the pond into the below-ground ice house and packing it with sawdust. Neighbor men, all bundled up in warm clothing and with extra pairs of gloves, came to help. Dad had ice spuds and saws and several sets of ice tongs. Some brought additional equipment. Some-one built and tended a fire in a barrel at the pond's edge. The barrel was a popular spot to visit and joke as they warmed themselves during the day.

One of the hired men harnessed Jack and Kate and hitched them to a low ice sled. They backed the sled near to the edge of the ice as men began to chop holes with axes or ice spuds. When a large enough hole was ready, the men sighted the lengths and widths for the cuts and began to saw. It was hard to get the first chunk out and up onto the surface. They pulled it with ice tongs onto a slippery "bridge board," between pond and sled, taking care not to let it get dirty.

Loading the sled had to be done just right. Sometimes there was snow, sometimes frozen earth. Either way, those mules had to squat down low in their traces and pull together with all their might to get the load started up the slope to more level ground. The men walked behind the sled and the steam blew out of the mules' noses because it was an incline for about the first 20 yards.

Dad cleaned the ice house before "putting up" the day's ice and spread a new layer of fresh sawdust (free from saw mills) to cover the dirt floor. The door was barely big enough to crawl through, but two men went down inside the dark room and arranged the ice blocks in neat rows, leaving a space between blocks so they wouldn't freeze together. A thick layer of sawdust on top kept the ice from melting. The door was sealed and all cracks closed at the end of the hard day's work. Later Dad would go help the neighbors fill their ice houses on another cold day.

Some farmers went without ice when the supply was gone, but Dad had a retail dairy and had to buy manufactured ice in town when his supply was gone. A 300-pound block cost a dollar and it took at least half a chunk per day.

When the sultry days of summer came, I'd crawl down into that dark pit, feeling my way down the ladder. Soon my eyes adjusted to the dimness, but the door had to be closed behind me and the only light came through the cracks around the door and where the roof touched the ground. I'd enjoy the damp, cool comfort until I'd screech when some toad would touch me with his cold body or some lizard-like ground puppy would scamper over my bare foot. They, too, liked the natural air conditioning.

It was a sad day for me when Dad said, "I'm not putting up ice this year, we'll just buy it."

He needed the space for the new milk house he was building. He tore down the ice house roof and filled in the pit with broken milk bottles, rusted cans, rocks, old tires, fence wire, and other historical trash from O.D. Meyers's dairy farm and home—maybe even the ice saws? I'd like to be the archaeologist who finds that buried treasure. It may now be in some family's front yard, you know.

Testing Dad's really great melons about 1923.

"BOOSIASMS"

When Mother was a young lady, her priorities included stylish clothing, piano playing, vocal music, cooking and embroidery. Nancy Henry was little more than five feet tall and weighed 90 pounds when she fell head over heels in love with a poor farmer with only an eighth-grade education. Orlando Denver Meyers was not a good catch. His mother died in childbirth when "Lando" was only four years old. He went to school with his half sisters because there were no sitters and so Susie, Mamie, Edy and Rose were the only "mother" he ever knew. His schooling ended at age 14 but Dad kept learning all of his 81 years. After he and Nancy married, he looked to her for lots of answers because she had the advantage of a high school education. More importantly, he worshipped her!

This tiny young woman put on a lot of weight after marriage, but Dad always said, "That's the way I like it. Who'd buy a skinny old horse or cow with its ribs sticking out?" Buxom was the term for women like Mom. Even so, she loved to hike in the woods and across the branch to visit her friend Bess Estes. Mom and Bess exchanged recipes and quilt patterns. They shared their newly made preserves or garden vegetables and Mom often took magazines or newspapers because Bess's family didn't have a phone or a car.

Bess and many of Mom's other friends were also heavyset women. Their husbands worked hard, had good appetites and ate lots of pork. They liked potatoes, eggs and fish fried in lard. Everybody seasoned green beans and other garden vegetables with bacon fat. No wonder so many women were obese and euphemistically called "stout," "heavyset" or "buxom." They cooked and ate what their husbands liked to eat.

Many women carried handkerchiefs or other tiny objects in the convenient place just under their chins—their "boosiasms," (pronounced boo-zee-as-ums). Bra and brassiere are newer words describing "a garment controlling and shaping the female breasts," but boosiasm was the cozy, cuddly word popular in my youth. Mom always carried Dad's gold watch there when we walked to Bess Estes's house. There were few treasures from Dad's family so the gold watch was especially important to all of us.

One evening when we reached home, the watch was gone! "I had it at Bess's house," Mom said. "I checked the time just before we started home." We searched the path till dark but found no watch. Dad consoled Mom by saying, "You didn't lose it on purpose" but Mom vowed that we'd find it.

The next day we walked the path again and, when hopping across the little branch, Mom spied the precious watch face up in the water! With a scream of joy, she retrieved the family treasure and discovered that it was ticking away, keeping perfect time. It was a happy day.

OLD DOC SHAFER

One day when I was a preschooler, my Mom rushed me to the doctor because I'd swallowed a penny. She probably knew that Dr. Shafer wasn't the only doctor in the world, but I didn't know that. He was "the doctor" and he lived between our house and town. He usually saw us at his home, as was the case when I swallowed the penny.

Dr. Shafer first comforted Mom and then he looked in my mouth and said, "It'll likely take care of itself. Let's wait." But Mom wasn't satisfied with that simple treatment, so Shafer said we'd have an X-ray.

That X-ray cost five dollars! One of the earliest joys that I can recall was knowing that my parents thought enough of me to justify their spending all of that money on ME! Self esteem set in, right then. Until that day I'd been "Little Miss Nobody." I was tiny, the second child, the girl, my brother's little sister.

Suddenly I took on new importance in the neighborhood. Mom related the incident to her friends who were my friends' mothers. People swarmed around me at Olivet Church a few days later to hear about the rushed trip and the X-ray. "Did it hurt?" they asked.   "Could they see inside your body with a camera?" And, "Did the X-ray get the penny out?"

The penny, of course, had been forgotten, but not the incident. I'd never been so important in all four or five years of my life!

Recently I was looking in the yellow pages of the Columbia telephone directory so I could call my "skin man." I stopped to count how many of my "men" (and women) there are. There's the bone man, ear man, throat man, dentist, heart man, eye man, the GYN, surgeons for this and that, lab technicians, the people who put patients to "sleep" and of course, my doctor.

Having this large medical staff doesn't exactly relate to the fact that I'm old. A younger person might need additional physicians for infectious diseases, growing pains, child psychiatry, adolescent medicine or otorhinolaryngology, whatever that is.

Thumbing through 10 pages in GTE's 1987 "Guide to Physicians and Surgeons," the thought struck me: suppose one of my little grandsons swallows a penny. Would I call someone listed in gastrointestinal endoscopy? Or thoracic surgery or radiology or pediatric surgery or internal medicine or otorhinolaryngology?

None of these individuals lives between my house and town and I don't call any of them by their first name. I'd be more shook up than was my dear old Mom. Perhaps I'd first call my cardiologist and have him prescribe something to calm me down. I might use the "wait and see" technique that worked so well in 1919. 🐄

BURNOUT

MAY 18, 1922

My brother and I rode to town in the milk truck that morning and Arthur Williams, the delivery man, dropped us off at school. Jim was in second grade and I was in first. It was Mom's wash day and she was taking the dirty clothes to her laundry room at the milk house when we left. The steam boiler there provided constant hot water. Dad had hitched up the mules and filled the planter boxes with seed corn.

Dad was planting in the southwest field when he glanced skyward and saw smoke! "OH! GOD, NO!" Black smoke boiled up from between the six maple trees that surrounded our home. He leaped off the planter and ran toward the house in knee high rubber boots. He was thinking, *"Get help! Get things out."* Dad often retold these things, always with hurt in his face. Heavier clouds of smoke rolled skyward. When he reached the barn he screamed, "Fire! The house! Help me!" and he kept on running. The hired men thought he'd lost his mind and went back to their work.

One shotgun blast and then another. Then a barrage as a whole box of shells exploded. They were near the back door so

Dad went to the front door. He held his breath and rushed into thick smoke in the living room. *"Damn that big chair."* He'd get the library table, our valuable papers were in its drawer. He dragged the table to the door but had to have air. He yanked the big chair out of the way again as he stumbled outside. The solid oak table had a long narrow drawer containing deeds and other papers. Groping in the smoke, he found the table and pulled it toward the door. *"Get air!"*

Going back, he yanked at the table till a leg came off. The heat was unbearable. Back for air! He got the drawer out and held the papers so nothing would be lost. He couldn't go in again. Exhausted and crazed, he collapsed against a big tree suffering, wondering, dreading for Mom to return.

He saw two men carrying hams out of the smokehouse. *"The meat!"* he thought as he ran. *"And Nancy's canned goods are in that cellar."* Wisps of smoke and tiny flames were breaking through the roof. He made one trip in, untwisted baling wires and saved some cured bacon slabs. To Joe and Leslie, he demanded, "Stay out! The roof is going in." Joe Baumgartner and Les Wegener had seen the smoke from Fulton Gravel Road. Others were coming by then. Someone heard the distress call. "Central" screamed repeatedly, "O. D. and Nancy's house is on fire!"

We were coming down Crouch's hill when Mother pulled the gas lever down hard and screamed, "That's my house!" We were a mile away and home was not in sight, but Mom knew.

We saw the walls fall in just as we crested the hill. Dad met us and he and Mom held each other tight for a long time. They grabbed Jim and me and held us close as we cried together. Finally Mom wiped her face and said, "Don't cry. We're all safe and we'll get through this somehow." Then neighbors and friends crowded around offering help and sympathy. Our lawn was washed by many tears that day!

There had been no fire of any kind in the house on that laundry day – except the little oil flame that kept about a hundred chicken eggs warm in the incubator – just a wall away from those shotgun shells which exploded early.

What did we have left? A library table drawer and its contents, a Morris chair with one cushion and Grandmother Henry's embroidered towel, which was damp when Mom took the other clothes off the line. She had gathered the dry pieces and piled them on her bed before leaving to pick Jim and me up from school. But the most important thing we had left was abundant love for each other and for our friends.

Dad hitched the team to the big iron cookstove and pulled it from the warm ashes. We scraped that stove inside and out. They set it under the maple tree at the corner of the garden and Mom cooked on it for almost five months! There was a sweet smell around the rubble. My folks had laid in 200 pounds of sugar for making jelly, preserves and jam, and it bubbled and caramelized for more than a week where the sacks had been stored in the kitchen.

We wept at the sight of Mom's piano – more than a hundred twisted and broken strings were sticking out in all directions. We knew there'd be no money to replace the piano for years to come.

When the ashes cooled we probed for treasures: broken pieces of Grandma Henry's Haviland plates, a silver spoon given to Mom by her Sunday School class, Dad's gold watch with no hands or face, never to run again, and the runners from our sled that we had kept under the house.

The Crouch family took us to their home for several days and loaned Jim and me clothing to wear to school the following day. Mrs. Pace hosted a huge miscellaneous shower. Mrs. Lynes gave Mom a good old Wheeler and Wilson sewing machine. A man loaned us a large army tent and two cots. Someone sent a big bed with springs and mattress. Edna Pace gave me a favorite doll. I was quite touched by that. A year and a half later the Pace's house also burned to the ground and Mom hosted a shower for her. I gave Edna the most important gift of my life. I had picked and stemmed a gallon of wild gooseberries and sold them for two 50-cent coins—one dollar! I gave Edna half of all my wealth—a silver half dollar. I never felt so good about anything before, or since.

I was six when this burnout changed our lives. When my own children were old enough to grasp the horror of the event, we went over to the area and I told them, "This is where we lived. These big rocks walled up our well..." Then I reminisced about how not many farm women had a sink and drain in the kitchen like Mom had and a well right on the back porch. I knew when it was Saturday because Mom would put the wash tub in the front yard and carry buckets of cold water and a tea kettle of boiling hot water and give me a bath. Then it was Jim's turn. She always fixed us soft-boiled eggs and crumbled crackers to mix in them. Then she'd put us to bed early. She and Dad would take turns bathing after dark, adding a kettle of hot water to the used water for each bather. When the bath routine started, I'd ask Mom, "Is the lightning coming again?" And it often did, from May till early October, in 1922.

"The big iron cooking range was here," I told them. "Mom

put the baby chickens here when they hatched in the incubator and weren't able to go into the brooder house yet." I told my kids how frightening lightning is when viewed from inside a wet tent by a six-year-old child who is awakened in the night. "I have never forgotten the sky streaks and horrible thunder of those storms," I told them. "It was as vivid as if we'd been sleeping outdoors and almost as wet, too. Water blew in at the tent flaps and the seams would drip water on our bedclothes.

"Some nights there was almost no dry place in my bed, which was a canvas cot with a very hard stick going crossways under my back." Mom and Dad studied the catalogs far into the night for two weeks. They finally borrowed money from the bank and ordered a Redi-Cut from the Aladdin Company in Bay City, Michigan. It was a five-room white frame bungalow with an indoor BATH!

"Up until that time, Aunt Ella Henry gave me the only bath I ever had in a real tub," I said. The kids giggled at that.

Cold weather made us move into the new home before the inside partitions and finish work were done. "Mother was constantly sweeping shavings and stacking saw horses in one end of the long living room at night," I told them.

By faith and hard work, Mom and Dad began the long climb back. We were deeply in debt, the price of milk was down, we needed to buy almost everything and it all cost more than we could afford. It seemed, however, that our crisis was over the day Dad surprised Mom with a "new" used piano he'd found for $50.

Remembering Mom's music, our new home, the way we all worked together that year and the years to follow – and my telling Nancy and Walt about it – gave us all a new respect for my parents' courage, faith and diligence in the face of seemingly insurmountable odds. I shall not forget that hour of remembering. Perhaps it changed my children's lives in some way too.

The music center in our new house. To the right is the only chair we saved from the fire.

CHILD ON THE FARM

Jim and me, 1916.

OUR ALADDIN REDI-CUT HOUSE

I really enjoyed living in the big tent that we borrowed after our house burned in the spring of 1922. I was only six years old and it seemed like a great adventure. Dad and Mom knew that we needed permanent shelter by cold weather, so they stayed up late reading catalogs and finally chose an Aladdin Redi-Cut House made in Bay City, Michigan. It was shipped in on the Wabash freight car and several neighbors helped haul the lumber, big buckets of paint, kegs of nails and endless instructions for erecting the home.

John Estes worked regularly on the house, and the milk house crew helped in the middle of the day, but only one professional carpenter was on the job. Uriel Evans, a member of our church, was employed to hang doors and windows. Mom was so thrilled when they fitted the kitchen cabinets. They assembled them in the dining room and carried them to their marked off place. The Aladdin Company even allowed for the thickness of the plaster. Many curious people came to view this Redi-Cut home and we were very proud.

By early October it was getting cold in the tent, so Mom and

Dad cleared out the new home and we moved in. Studding
indicated where the rooms were going to be, but we could walk
through closets, halls and rooms because the walls were not in
place.

Sweeping sawdust and shavings kept us busy each night as
we made the house livable for the four of us. Nobody really
cared. It was such a novelty to have a home again. We had
never had big windows, a furnace, a basement or a fireplace!
The toilet and bath were luxuries beyond my imagining. I still
like the fragrance of fresh curls of wood and the clatter of
hammers! 🚲

Charlotte Stradford's painting includes our 1938 Dodge dairy truck,
our three-legged dog Jiggs, the water tower, carbide light equipment, and even the stain from motor oil that ran down the driveway
the day Mom drove too close to a 50-gallon barrel in the garage.

"A FOOL AND HIS MONEY ARE SOON PARTED"

Dad gave me a whole half dollar when we went to the annual Fourth of July picnic at a huge pasture east of town. "You don't have to spend it," he'd say. Mom would add, "You could save some for another time." Dad and Mom had a lot of good advice. "Throw things away where you can find them later," Dad said, especially during the Depression. "Gambling doesn't pay," Mom said. And they taught me that "A fool and his money are soon parted."

This Elks' Picnic half dollar was mine, however, to keep or spend as I wanted. One time each year, I was allowed the freedom of racing around with my friends, spending BIG money. This picnic was a sort of carnival. We'd check out the whole pasture full of fun things and then buy an ice cream cone for a nickel and lick it as we walked back to whatever booth or stand we liked the best. People were throwing balls at dolls, turning clicking wheels and tossing coins at a target on a board. Other people were raking the money in with a stick or handing out huge, gaudy lamps and dolls and things. Everywhere people were having fun and some were even winning money.

I remember one special Elks' Picnic when I was in grade school. There were hundreds of American flags flying and patriotic bunting was draped over a speakers' stand. Men in red vests and straw sailor hats played the loudest music I'd ever heard, and there were glass bottles of red "sody pop" to suck up through a straw! Men yelled through megaphones to get people to come to their booths. I vividly remember one man who kept calling, "Dollar and a half box of candy for a dime." I watched as several men carefully rolled golf balls down troughs on a flat table. Eight or ten fellows took turns rolling the balls. The expensive box of candy went to the one who could make the ball touch the end of the trough, roll back and stop nearest to a red line. It looked easy! The fellow with the megaphone didn't even look at me when I extended my dime for a chance to roll the ball. I was crushed. I'd never tasted "dollar and a half chocolates" and I was anxious to make that ball stop at the red line. On tip toes, I finally got the man's attention and "bought" a chance to roll. When he got enough dimes to have all of the troughs busy, we took turns rolling.

I wouldn't be telling this if I hadn't been the winner! My friends, and all those men watching, cheered me on. I sold the candy for five dimes and rolled again on the next round. And the next! I didn't win every time I rolled, but I went home happy. I had red "sody" stains on my blouse, a box of chocolates under one arm and my pockets heavy with dimes!

My parents had a few strong words about little girls who gamble, but they smiled at each other when they started to say, "A fool and his money are ..."

JOE GARITY AND
THE GIFT OF ICE SKATES

Joe Garity was walking through Missouri to no place in particular during the time when Fulton Gravel Road was the shortest route between New York City and Los Angeles. He waited until Dad's day's work was winding down and then asked for a job. He was neatly dressed, polite and unfamiliar with what goes on at a busy dairy farm. Dad, however, needed an extra hired hand and he figured Joe was hungry, had no place to sleep and could surely learn to wash milk cans and things like that.

"I pay a dollar and a half a day and your keep," Dad said. "We could give you supper and a bed and then see what we can work out tomorrow."

Joe agreed to that. He stayed in our unfinished attic room and we accepted him as one of the family. Mom did his laundry and mending.

Joe fit in from the first. We five would play Flinch after supper or Mom would play the piano and we'd all sing. He didn't tell us when he had a birthday, didn't write or get letters or use the telephone. The only identification he ever gave was that he had a sister in Scranton, Pennsylvania. If he carried any extra clothes, they weren't for work because he used his first week's pay to buy bib overalls and blue shirts like the other men wore.

Three years later he had bought a wonderful Silvertone radio and some lesser gifts for our family and an old car for himself. We'd huddle around that morning glory speaker and get WLS and KDKA stations. My world was extending beyond the farm and the town four miles away.

The winter of the big snow and ice storm, the men hunted up some rusty Keen Kutter ice skates which clamped onto the thick soles of their shoes. They sharpened them and were skating everywhere! The six-inch snow was covered with a thick layer of ice and we had some great slopes for skating. My shoes wouldn't hold those clamps and I'd never had skates. On pay day Joe went to Hays Hardware and bought me a pair of brand new ice skates that had leather straps at the heels. Wow! That was about the greatest thing I'd had happen to me!

We'd start at the steep incline in front of the house and fly downhill. I learned to slow down and squat low to get under a two-strand barbed wire fence and to hop across a little branch and then skate up the hill on the opposite side. Little things like that change a kid's whole life.

My own children have never had a chance to skate over the pastures and we don't welcome ice over snow, but we've skated on ponds and creeks a lot. Big Cedar creek is near our farm and my friend Petie and her son, Jimmy, went there with us one very cold day. Nobody remembers much about the skating that day when the children were grade school age. We built a good fire and the kids set sticks on fire and played like they were sparklers.

I looked at Petie and she looked at me. Should we tell about grape vines? We smiled silently and told the youngsters to hunt up some dry, wild grape vines. Soon all five of us were "smoking" those hollow vines and trying to blow smoke rings. We knew we risked starting our kids on a bad habit. Not to worry! They accepted it for what it was—their moms reliving some fun things they did in childhood. 🚲

MY BEST
FISHING,MEMORY

The day that Dad quit working long enough to take the family and hired men fishing is one of the happiest memories of my childhood.   Dad was a busy dairy farmer and there was always more work than he could get done.   But on this day we went to the creek with a length of chicken wire and two poles to seine for creek perch and catfish.

While this is probably illegal now, back then it produced enough fish for us to invite the neighbors over for supper.   The memory of that wonderful day is topped by the fact that the trip was all Dad's idea.   If we'd stayed home to do the work, no one would have remembered it.   Going off together to have fun brought me happiness that has not dimmed through the years.

YELLOWAY TRAGEDY IN 1926

The extension of East Broadway, which is now named Route WW, was first called Boone's Lick Trail, then Cedar Creek Road and, in 1926, Fulton Gravel Road. It was the shortest route between New York City and Los Angeles. The first coast-to-coast busses traveled this narrow, winding gravel road. One of the first was the "Yelloway" bus line.

In 1924, during a virtual "cloudburst," creeks went beyond their banks on the Fulton Gravel Road. At about two in the morning, a Yelloway bus loaded with 28 passengers was plying its way down a long hill on its way to Columbia. Down at the foot of the hill, the road made a sharp right turn onto a narrow iron bridge over Grindstone Creek. When the driver made that turn, the huge yellow bus plunged headlong into the rampaging waters! He had missed the bridge! The front part of the bus was submerged and passengers were thrown forward into the part of the bus which was rapidly filling with water. Miraculously, the driver and all but two of the passengers survived.

Two families lived near enough to hear the screams of frightened and injured persons. Someone cranked that party line ringer frantically. Every phone on the line rang. That brought several people out of bed to see what had happened. Other people got the message from "Central," and men headed to the scene of the accident. Women stayed on the line and talked together about who could take some of the frightened, wet people into their homes. They made coffee and sandwiches and waited for unexpected guests.

My parents, almost a mile away, rushed to the scene in the dairy truck, while others went by car or horse and buggy. They took coal oil lanterns and blankets. Some took bed sheets with which to make slings or bandages.

Passengers escaped through the back windows into the roaring waters. Some were washed downstream and into pastures and fields. Sadly, a little child and an older man were dead. The rescuers knew that their first job was to help the living. They offered transportation and took those frightened and injured people into their homes, fed them and gave them warm beds.

By dawn the creeks were back in their banks. People wandered around in the mud, trying to find their lost belongings. Dad and Carl Hobart, found hats, books, shoes, billfolds, purses and other personal items for the next several days. They took them to the bus depot to be returned to their owners.

Mom, Dad and their friends often talked about the Yelloway bus tragedy. Many victims and their rescuers established friendships which lasted through the years. 🚲

SASSAFRAS!
NOW THERE'S A CUP O' TEA

A pleasant surprise for the first settlers was that Indians taught them to grub out the roots of sassafras trees, scrub them and boil them to make a delicious cup of tea. Indians used it as a medicine for a variety of ailments and our forefathers said it was a good spring tonic "to thin the blood." Most people found it aromatic and delicious. Large quantities of the wood were shipped from the colonies to Europe where it was accepted for its flavor and aroma but not as a medicine.

Forty years ago we could buy a little bundle of sassafras sticks in most produce sections of our grocery stores. That ended in the 1960's when it was discovered that the oil of sassafras was toxic, a hazard to our health. In large quantities it might even be a carcinogen.

When I was a kid hunting and digging sassafras roots was a great excuse to go strolling in the woods on a warm spring day. Later, as a leader of a 4-H project in which boys and girls learned to used native materials, we made place mats out of the hated broom sedge weed, bookends out of selected stones from the creek and small trays and beads out of clay we dug from the ground. As a money making project we went to the woods with grubbing hoes and axes and dug sassafras roots. We left the bark on the roots and scrubbed them clean. Then the boys sawed the roots into three-inch lengths and split them into little finger-sized sections. After a final scrubbing, we bundled these and sold them to Eastgate Grocery. We didn't make a lot of money but we had a lot of fun in the woods on early spring days.

A member of the laurel family, sassafras is found only in the middle and eastern United States and in southern Canada. All parts of the tree are aromatic; the leaves and twigs were sometimes processed into an ingredient in soups. The flavoring has also been used in medicines, candy and in beverages such as root beer before it was taken off the commercial market. A concentrated liquid called "Sassafras flavoring" was bottled and sold for a short time, but it too disappeared from grocery shelves.

Whatever our feeling about the uses of sassafras, pure joy awaits us as we tramp through the woods on a warm spring day, grubbing hoe in hand, hunting the right tree. We'll break twigs and sniff them and look nearby for fallen leaves that are ovals with a "thumb" notch on one side like a mitten. Better yet, we can think ahead and mark some sassafras trees in summer before the leaves fall.

Locate a sassafras tree and then dig the roots which spread out wide and not terribly deep in the ground. The roots have a more distinct fragrance than the leaves, bark or twigs. After a final scrubbing with a stiff brush, rinse them and put five or six root pieces in a quart of water and simmer it until the fragrance fills the room and the liquid is pink. Pour it through a tea strainer or cheesecloth, add sugar, stir and enjoy the drink our ancestors thought was essential in Spring, for thinning the blood. The harder the roots are to come by, the better the tea will taste. If you don't believe it, ask any old timer. 🚲

Bess, Sally, Linda, and Susan dig Sassafras roots

PLANE IN THE CLOUDS

George Williams was born one year before I was; his whole family worked for Dad and Mother at one time or another. George was hoeing corn with Dad when airplanes were scarce—something to stare at. They stopped and leaned on their hoes and Dad said, "George, you watch. That plane will go into that cloud on this side and come out on the other." George watched. When the plane reappeared he said, "Ya' know, Boss, I don't believe that!" ⚲

GRINDING CORN

On Saturday mornings when I was just a little kid, the chore I loved most was driving Jake around the corn grinder. I sat up on that big horse which Dad hitched to the end of a long pole, the grinder "tongue." As Jake walked around in circles, the corn settled down into the grinder's burrs, was crushed to the right size for cow feed and dropped into an old bent wash tub. Around the grinder, the horse's big hooves had made a wide, bare circle about two inches deep.

The grinder stood near the corn storage bin from which Dad would throw scoops of ear corn into the noisy crusher. I'd walk Jake around and around, keeping the old horse on the move until the tub was full. Because it was ear corn, the cobs were crushed too, which provided roughage for the cows. When the wash tub was full, Dad emptied it into feed sacks, tied them shut and loaded them onto the wagon to be hauled to the dairy barn. We always kept out a bucketful for Mom's chickens.

To make Dad's special blend of feed for his 30 Holstein milk cows, he'd start with chop and then add bright yellow cotton seed meal and wheat bran from the Boone County Milling

Company in town. Then he'd sprinkle a dash of salt over the pile. He'd take the scoop and mix the ingredients until none of the bright yellow cotton seed meal showed up. He'd use corn silage with this combination of ingredients, which he learned was the best mixture for his Holstein herd.

Helping with the grinding of ear corn gave me a feeling of having a part in the dairy operation. I knew how to do something that needed to be done. Having a responsibility as simple as riding a horse that couldn't go anywhere but in a circle still made me feel good about myself. I was actually sorry when modern machinery replaced Jake and me. 🚲

OUR WRECK DIDN'T STOP THE CHRISTMAS PROGRAM

We'd been at Olivet Church all afternoon, practicing for the Christmas program. Then we drove to the home of Ethel and Alec Scheurer for our annual get together, a week before Christmas. Herschel and Marjorie Scheurer were about our ages so my brother and I really looked forward to this celebration. Their brother, John Jay, was younger.

We ate Christmas dinner, visited and sang carols until after 11 p.m. It was a cold calm night and as we were driving home on Range Line gravel road, the Model T car sputtered as if it weren't getting enough gas. Dad leaned far over to the right to reach the end of a rod that led to the carburetor. Wham! Bang! Crash!

Our two seated Ford touring car had crashed and turned upside down in the roadside ditch. Mom was badly hurt and bleeding profusely. Dad shouted, "Jim, go get Alec and the buggy." Jim took off running fast.

In the darkness, it was difficult to determine the extent of Mom's injuries. Dad sat on the ground, comforting her and gently pressing something over her face to control the bleeding.

I recall that I wept but stifled the urge to bawl out loud. I had never seen anyone injured like this. Jim and Dad, who were in the front seat, were shaken up but not hurt and my problem began about an hour later.

It was more than a quarter of a mile back to Scheurer's and they didn't own a car. Alec hurriedly bundled up, lit a coal oil lantern, harnessed the horse and hitched it to the buggy. It seemed as if we waited for hours but finally we heard the clop, clopping of the horse's hooves and the crunch of buggy wheels on gravel. Help had come! Herschel and Marjorie ran along behind the buggy.

The lantern light revealed that the bleeding had stopped and my mother had the most horrible looking bloody face I had seen in all of my ten years! Dad and Alec helped Mom into the buggy and she leaned on Alec as he drove slowly on the bumpy gravel road. Dad and we four kids walked behind. My back was aching and I couldn't keep up with the others as they followed the buggy. Soon I had to walk bending forward to ease the pain and Marjorie walked along with me.

Ethel sponged Mom's face and put her to bed. We all stayed two nights. The men studied the wrecked car and determined that the crash was caused by a bent radius rod. Dad had lost control when he reached to adjust the gas. The right front wheel dropped into a washed out place in the road, bending the radius rod and causing the crash. The wooden bow that held the canvas top in place splintered and poked Mom in the face in two places. One laceration was in her forehead above her eye and the other was inside the eye socket. The latter one could have completely destroyed her eye.

Swelling, bruising and lacerations; what a sight she was the next day! She treated her wounds with Tincture of Iodine, a yellow liquid which stung a lot, smelled bad and was an old standby to promote healing and prevent infection.

In spite of the fact that the swelling and bruises still distorted her face a week later, Mom played for the Christmas program as planned. I was well by then.

What did the doctor do for Mom? Nothing! She didn't see her doctor. Iodine healed her but she had a scar on her forehead that lasted a lifetime.

Walt and Norma Sapp Frasier won first prize in the New Haven School costume contest.

HALLOWEEN RAG-BAG COSTUMES

In the fall of the year, we whispered to our grade school friends, "What'cha going to be this year?" Most of us scrounged for Halloween costumes in the family rag bag. It's amazing how many different looking ghosts, hoboes, witches and bag ladies came out of those rag bags.

Dad's theory about old stuff was, "Throw it away where you can find it. You may wish you had it later." He and Mom were short and heavyset so their discarded clothes were about the right length and could be stuffed with pillows to make witches and goblins. Old sheets and a handful of safety pins created wonderful ghosts. We made false faces out of brown grocery bags, using bright colored yarn for hair and drawing in the mouth, nose and eyes.

On party day, we'd roll up our rag-bag costumes and stuff them in a sack. After the last bell rang, we'd scatter and hide to put on our garbs. What an array of creatures appeared! Only my best friend knew which one I was at the school party.

To make a black cat costume for a school play, Mom used her long black cotton stockings to cover my arms and stuffed a third one with rags to make a tail. She bought the black cat mask. Our neighbor Ethel said, "When she gets dressed up in that cat suit, come down and show me." About dark on the day of the play, I dressed up, cat mask and all, and scratched on Ethel's door "meowing" in a strange voice. Ethel's husband, Alex, who was quite superstitious, cracked the door to see what was making those weird noises. Bang! He slammed it shut! I scratched and meowed again. Alex cracked the door and jabbed at me with a broomstick so I swung around to avoid being poked. Then he saw the big, heavy tail.

Alex made a quick getaway but I heard Ethel say, "Alex, it's Sue! It's just Sue dressed up!" I stood there wondering whether to run or knock again. Suddenly the door opened wide and Alex threw a bucket of water on me! I jumped back, quickly pulling off my mask, but it was limp and streaks of black ran down my face. Alex was so sorry and I was able to dry out enough to go on with the performance at school. Later he said, "It was that big black tail that scared me."

Our kids made costumes from the rag bag too. One year Nancy created the Mad Hatter without my help. The hat was more than two feet tall, made with blue poster paper, and it came down almost to her knees. She wore her brown tights and my shoes. Walt wanted to go as a headless man. We covered half of a cylindrical oatmeal box with skin colored strapping tape for the headless neck. I mounted this in a pillow which made shoulders. He put on Chub's shirt and tie over the neck and peeked out between the shirt buttons. My long all-weather coat completed the outfit, which almost dragged the ground.

As for me, I can still smell that damp paper-mâché mask that I wore in my school play many years ago. 🚲

HOGGING CATFISH

Mudcats I have known include dozens, maybe hundreds, of those bewhiskered fellows we caught in a neighbor's creek back in the 1920s. We ate some and put most in a pond on our dairy farm to be caught, released, and recaught many more times. Our catch might be a "big one," 11 or 12 inches long or a darling little caramel-colored fingerling that was not as long as the worm he swallowed. I remember the biggest catfish I ever saw. Believe me, he was no kitten!

Worms were the only bait we knew as kids and they worked just fine for mudcats, perch and an occasional "line striper" bass. The largest cats I had seen were the few which "the men" (my Dad and his friends) caught illegally by "hogging" them barehanded out of Perche Creek. It took courage which I didn't have, to wade deep, feeling under rocks and slimy ledges. I wondered why it was illegal to hog fish when it was done by so few. Watching from shore, I fully expected someone to come up with a water moccasin or at least with a big turtle snapped to his fingers.

Hogging was the best way to get fish enough for a community fish fry. We'd go west of town to Perche Creek. Mom, Jim and I would tie cane poles lengthwise to the top of the car and we'd fish from the bank with fat worms we'd dug by turning over planks and big rocks in the barn lot. Women who weren't fishing would spread out tablecloths and sort out the cooking supplies while the rest of us fished.

Occasionally the preacher and his family went along on these hogging trips. There was the time when Les Wegener located "a hell of a big cat" beneath an underwater rock ledge. He cussed loudly when it got away. At the same time, deacon Alex Scheurer had his hand on one. His hat floated off as he reached very deep to finally get his fingers in that big fish's mouth and his thumb in the gill. "Goddamnsonsabitch! He's gone!" Alex yelled, forgetting that the minister was present.

Before long, the preacher quietly lifted a five-pound catfish out of the water and said, "Boys, this is the kind you get if you don't cuss 'em." What a beauty! It was a message I'll never forget. 🚲

MY FIRST BIKE CHANGED MY LIFE

Elizabeth's father rescued an old damaged bicycle from the trash pile and got it into usable condition. We rode it on the trails at their farm. It was a direct-drive style with no brake and the pedals spun as fast as the wheels. Going down hills we'd spread our feet out wide and let 'er roll, hoping to land without crashing. It's hard to describe the exhilaration I felt on that bike. I was flying with wind in my face and I loved it! I determined that I had to have a bike of my own.

My brother's bike was too tall for me but I learned to ride it "standing up" with my right leg stuck under the bar to reach the right-side pedal.

I offered my $1.75 savings and told Dad, "I'll work for nothing for the next five years," if he'd buy the bike I had chosen from the Sears and Roebuck "wish book." He'd have to sell a lot of milk to afford a $39.95 bike. I wore the catalog pages to a ragged softness looking at "my" bike. Finally he told Mom to order it.

The day the big flat box arrived I was in seventh heaven! It was beautiful—tan and beige with white pinstripes and fat tires.

None of us had ever seen a brand new bike before. I watched as Dad assembled it in the dining room while Mom cleared the table after supper. When he started to put on the pedals, he got a strange look on his face. He attached the one marked "R" for the right side and then picked up the other. Oops! Both pedals were marked "R." There was no pedal for the left side!

There stood my dream-come-true, but with only one pedal. It would be at least a week before the wrong pedal could be returned to Kansas City and the correct one shipped back to Columbia. This was the most disappointing thing that had ever happened in all of my nine years!

I found I could sit on the seat and coast downhill, using the hub brake, and then walk up the steep grades. Mom and Dad approved my doing this on our half-mile-long driveway. But soon I was pulling the empty left crank around with my toe. I was a bird out of the nest, flying on my own power. This new mobility gave me confidence and self esteem. I now knew that I could do anything anyone else could do if I just tried. By the time the replacement pedal arrived, I hardly needed it.

The next summer, 1924, I bicycled to the First Baptist Church in Columbia to attend Bible School. Fulton Gravel Road was loose creek gravel but I rode it eight miles, five days a week, for two weeks.

At age 10, I realized that bicycling could enlarge my small world and make me happy for the rest of my life. And it has.

OPENING GATES FOR PAY

"Allowance" was not in our vocabulary when I was a kid. If we worked, we were paid—not much, of course, but something. It was taken for granted that I would help around the house because I was part of the family but when I washed milk bottles every day after school, I was a "hired hand." I was paid 25 cents a week and my world suddenly changed.

In 1928 torrential rains washed away the three bridges between our dairy farm and Columbia. I was employed by the Columbia Special Road District to open and close gates. I earned three times as much in a day as I made in a week washing milk bottles!

All of the floor boards washed away from the long iron bridge that spanned Hinkson Creek. Two other bridges were completely gone. Farmers used their mule teams and iron scrapers to make a detour around the place where Fulton Gravel road crossed the north fork of Grindstone creek.

At the crossing of Hominy Branch, Roy Mitchell gave permission for the Road District workmen to cut his fence, put in a gate and route traffic through his cow pasture. That meant that people had to go through a second gate. My job was to open and close those two gates to keep the cows and horses from getting out.

On the way to school in the milk truck, I'd open and close the first gate and then go down the steep incline where the bridge had been, hop across the water on some big rocks and climb the opposite bank to be at the next gate before the truck arrived. The road crew supervisor saw me do that and offered me the job on weekends.

Lucky me! No one said I couldn't take my fishing pole to work each day or that I had to shut a gate if the horses and cows weren't in sight. I took my fishing pole on that first Saturday and carried a tobacco can half full of worms in the big front pocket of my bib overalls. I hid them from one weekend till the next, near the deepest hole of water. I could watch the cows and horses and open the gates as needed without neglecting my work. Having fish was never the idea; catching them was my objective so I threw them back to catch again!

I knew most of the people who came along but a few strangers would offer me a nickel as a tip. At first I was embarrassed to accept it because I was making so much money and having so much fun with those little perch and mud cats. The embarrassment soon wore off and I enjoyed jingling those coins in my overall pockets. I didn't get to wear overalls on Sunday, I had to wear a dress.

One Saturday a stranger in a shiny Buick gave me a dime. The following week he returned on Sunday morning and gave me another dime saying, "I gave a little boy a dime here last week so I'll give you the same." Away he went while I pondered the ethics of not telling him that I was that "little boy!" 🚲

TONSILLECTOMY

Dr. Sumers's nurse called Mom the day before my scheduled tonsillectomy and asked, "How will you be coming down to Jefferson City tomorrow?" Mom told her she'd drive me over in the Model "T" touring car. "Bring a man's handkerchief along," she replied.

Now this was about 1924 and the best way to deal with tonsils that repeatedly became red and swollen was to get them out. I was a puny little thing and it was thought that a tonsillectomy would improve my general health. It cost about $50 in the hospital but Dr. Sumers did the work in his own office suite for half that.

Early the next morning, Mom, her friend Mary and I, made the long slow trip to Jeff City. When we entered the doctor's office, the nurse said, "Mrs. Meyers, I forgot to tell you that Sue shouldn't eat any breakfast; did she eat?" "Yes!" I had sort of tanked up because friends told me I'd have an awful sore throat after the surgery. As a result, I was left in a dark room to rest for about two hours to let my food digest.

I vividly recall when the nurse put a transparent mask over

my mouth and nose and I tried to keep from breathing that awful ether but soon felt that I was on a long slide, sailing down out of control. The next thing I knew the nurse was offering me some ice cream, saying, "You must be hungry." One bite and I was not hungry at all!

I sipped a little water and dropped off to sleep. In late afternoon, the nurse said, "Sue, you can go home now." That's where the man's handkerchief came in. "Hold this loosely over your nose all of the way home." Good advice. Every breath was like swallowing a sharp knife.

Dr. Sumers said, "Let her eat and drink anything she wants. Soda pop will be good to start with." Mom wrote the $25 check and gave me the folded handkerchief to hold over my face. We loaded into the open car and Mom cranked it for the long trip back on dusty gravel roads.

The next day Dad bought a whole case of soda pop. The first one I chose was cherry flavor. Mom popped off the cap and handed it to me. There was that knife in my throat again! By the second day I could swallow more comfortably. There was also strawberry, cream and orange to choose from and, to this day, cherry is my last choice.

By the time our own two children had frequent sore throats and inflamed tonsils, Dr. Garrett advised, "I think we should take them out." He removed several youngsters' tonsils each Friday, at Boone County Hospital. Nancy was the first one of ours to need this surgery. The date was set and arrangements made.

On Thursday, the day before she was scheduled to be at the hospital at 9:00 a.m., the nurse called to say, "Mrs. Gerard, I wonder if you realize that Nancy's tonsil operation is to be done on Friday the <u>thirteenth</u>?" No, I hadn't thought about it. "Dr. Garrett said that if this makes any difference to you, he'll be glad to change it."

I replied, "It doesn't make a particle of difference to me." And then I added, "I certainly hope it doesn't affect Dr. Garrett in any way!"

It didn't, of course, and by coincidence Walt's had to come out a few years later—on Friday the thirteenth! Perhaps there was a shortage of mothers to whom it made no difference? 🚲

Hattie Page and me, about 1935.

HATTIE PARSONS PAGE

Hattie was a nonconformist, an "old woman" on a University campus where almost no undergraduate students were past 25 years. She was the mother of my friend Catherine and had talked her way into the MU Journalism School. Her credentials were from a boarding school, yellowed and brittle. By age 38 she was the mother of three children and wife of a dirt farmer. But she was writing and selling articles to magazines and newspapers. She wanted to learn more.

When she was a student at a girls' school in Liberty, Missouri, she filled her own lamp with coal oil and trimmed its wick. She carried coal and tended the fire in a little stove in her dormitory room. The "facilities" were out back, reached by a path. For actual bathing, Hattie took a bucket to the well, pumped water, carried it to her room and heated it on the little stove. She poured hot water into a pitcher and bowl for her bath.

Hattie homesteaded in Oklahoma as a young single woman. By coincidence the homesteader on the adjacent land happened to be a bachelor. They married and later moved to a farm in our community. Their brick home was one of the first built in this part of Boone County. John Page was a gentle, slow-moving man who seemed generations older than his wife. Neighbors said, "By the time Page gets the team of horses to the end of a row, the corn has sprouted on the other end."

The Page home was a two-story brick structure built by Tom Turner and his slaves. They dug local clay for the bricks and burned limestone rocks from the creek and hillsides to make plaster for the walls. The Turners and their slaves fashioned beautiful old doors and other woodwork out of black walnut lumber from their woods. Hand-wrought hardware for the doors was of the "latchkey" design. Hattie cooked on a wood stove and sometimes made stew in an iron kettle over an open fire in the backyard.

My mother was Catherine Page's music teacher. On lesson day, Hattie would hitch the little brown pony to the open buggy for the four or five mile trip to our house. Hattie and Mom were good friends too. When it was time for the Pages to start home, Hattie would scoot around in the buggy seat and make room for me to ride about a mile and then I'd walk back.

The Pages bought two Italian-made violins for their sons, Bryant and William. William and I were friends too and, after his death at age 16, they gave me his violin. It was dark wood with three colorful decals on the back: a mountain scene, a lovely lady and some flowers. The label inside said that it was made by Carlo Bergonzi. Seeing my interest, my folks gave me 18 lessons from the orchestra leader at University High School.

Hattie was a fun person. Mundane chores didn't get in the way of her making taffy for Catherine and me or taking us to the creek for a swim or to fish. One Pie Supper Night at

Turner School near their home, they invited me to come stay all night so we could attend. I begged Mom to let me ride my new tan and cream colored Sears, Roebuck and Company bicycle to their home. Mom agreed and I started out about 4 p.m. Things went well on Fulton Gravel Road and I turned at the Carlisle School corner where gypsies often set up their wagons. I pushed the bike up a steep hill and rode on again to the next intersection. I turned left onto a less traveled road and there my problems began.

This road was wet and although creek gravel had been put in mud holes, the main tracks were sticky clay mud. I had to stop and dig the mud out from underneath the fenders of my new bike and then pedal on. Soon the sun set and the hedge trees on one side of the road made the going dark and difficult. I had to get off and dig the clay out so frequently that I wasn't making much progress at all. There were no others on the road at that time of day and nothing to be afraid of, but it was getting late and I didn't want to be late for the pie supper. When I discovered that the mud problem was almost all on the rear wheel, I began to guide the handlebars with my left hand and lift the rear wheel out of the mud with my right, which allowed me to move a bit faster. It became pitch dark and I heard the strange noise of an owl or something. It sounded like "O-u-u-u-ue," but I'd never heard it before. It was a long way off but getting closer. It puzzled me but I had work to do.

Was it an animal? A bird? Someone hurt? No, it was Hattie Page, slogging through the mud in four-buckle overshoes, calling, "Su-u-u-ue." We were really glad to see each other at that moment! She lifted the rear wheel out of the mud and carried it as I guided with both hands and we made good progress from then on. We were a little late for the pie supper. No one wanted my pie, so Mr. Page bought it and then he bought Catherine's too.

Hattie Parsons Page, next to my own parents, helped the most to shape my life. Just maybe it was her influence that caused me to choose the School of Journalism and enjoy writing? 🚲

CARBIDE GAS LIGHTS

It's hard to imagine not having electrical current to turn on lights, cool refrigerators, pump water for cattle, grind feed, light the way to our cars at night or even to power a simple radio. But electric lines in Mid-Missouri stopped at the city limits in the 1930s. Coal oil lamps and lanterns were a lot of trouble and gave surprisingly little light.

A few rural families owned Delco light plants, which were private generators powered by gasoline engines. They were, however, far from trouble free! Dad and Mom chose a different solution: carbide gas lights.

The carbide "plant" was a huge tank, mostly below ground level, in the side yard near our house. We bought granular carbide in 50-pound drums and poured that into one compartment. The granules sprinkled down into water, forming gas. A large metal float contained the gas until needed. Metal tubing went underground to the house, milk house and barn. Instead of light bulbs, there was a valve, a Y-shaped outlet and a striker. To ignite gas for lights or to heat an iron, I'd have to stretch up and turn a valve and then twist the striker. The spark of the striker ignited gas which came from the outlet.

This was far better than coal oil lamps and lanterns. No more filling and spilling that stinky kerosene. There were no smoky chimneys to wash and polish. While there was a certain amount of danger involved with an open flame in a lamp that could be tipped over while lighted, it never happened at our house. The main advantage of carbide was that it was good light that spread out over the entire room. There were some drawbacks, however.

The day the tubes and fixtures were in place and the carbide had formed its gas in the big outdoor tank, it was necessary to vent the tubes before the gas could be ignited. As instructed, we opened doors and windows and turned on the valves to let out the air. Only after all three of our canaries died did we realize that the carbide gas wasn't the best for human beings either. That taught us to turn and strike quickly so almost no gas would escape into the room.

The carbide ran out when we least expected. If it happened in the evening, the oil lanterns and lamps were pressed into service. It was possible to determine when a refill was necessary, but to do that we had to open the big tank and look in, and sometimes we'd forget to do that.

There was a spigot where Mom attached the flexible tube for her gas iron. She would open the iron, turn on the gas and wait for the tube to fill. Then she'd light the match and ignite the gas quickly, remembering those three dead canaries!

When the idea of a farmer-owned cooperative was set in motion, Dad was one of the volunteers who promoted the idea. Many farmers thought that they'd only need electricity for lights and maybe an iron for the wife. Dad knew better! 🚲

FOX WAS A
CHURCH GOIN' DOG

Mr. Crouch, one of my fifth grade teachers at the University of Missouri Laboratory School, asked me to stay after class one day. I don't remember a lot about him and I probably wasn't one of his best students, but he made my whole family happy that day when he said, "Sue, I have a nice little dog that I must give away. Since you live on a farm, I thought you might like to have him."

I liked the idea right then and Dad and Mom liked it too. Soon we brought the little white and black terrier to the farm to live with us. It was mutual love at first sight.

It didn't take long for Fox, a city dog, to take to the farm like a duck takes to water. He loved the freedom of not being fenced in and he went almost everywhere our family went, even to church. Other people's dogs also went to church. Some just trotted along with the horses if the family drove a buggy or surrey. People who lived within a mile of the church just walked and their dogs walked along.

Bill McHarg's big collie was as regular as clockwork because he lived right across the road from the church and he liked to be where the action was. When people began to congregate, he'd walk across Fulton Gravel Road over to Olivet Church and visit the other dogs. One morning he had been outside until the service started and, in a quiet moment after the hymn singing, the collie ambled down to the front of the sanctuary and plopped down on the soft rug in front of the pulpit. Fox never did anything like that. He went to church more for the ride than for the sermon.

Dad taught him to ride on the running board of our Ford touring car. But Fox taught himself to climb farther up on the left front fender, bracing against the car's hood. In that position he snapped constantly – at the wind or bugs or something. He rode and snapped that way for many miles and enjoyed it even when we went to see Aunt Rose, a drive of about two hours in each direction. Fox went right along on the fender.

One warm fall day, the Reverend R. C. Abram was in the middle of his sermon at Olivet when Fox suddenly burst through the open door. He ran down the aisle to a wooden music storage cabinet, barking and sniffing excitedly. Dad bounded out of his seat and grabbed Fox, trying to quiet him as he headed for the door. Brother Abram stopped him. "No, Mr. Meyers, come back. Let the little dog get that mouse that's been chewing up our music books and Sunday School literature."

By this time everyone in the congregation was standing and the room buzzed with quite a commotion. Bob Reid, chairman of the church board, hurried to the music cabinet to help with the hunt. It took only a moment. Reid cracked the cabinet door open, Dad put the anxious terrier down and he squeezed into the cabinet, then out he came with the wiggling, squealing

mouse clamped between his jaws, its tail flailing back and forth.
A roar of applause congratulated Fox as he held the squealing
mouse high while trotting down the aisle and out the door. I
know he enjoyed the extra attention he was getting. Fox had
done in a moment what traps had failed to accomplish.

The congregation sat down, the room became quiet and
Brother Abram picked up the sermon and continued as if nothing had happened.

Our city dog had adapted quite well to the country, even to
the country church. 🚲

Fox and me, about 1928.

STRING PHONES

We kids made a telephone using two tin cans and a long strong cord. It actually worked. We used a hammer and nail to punch a small hole in the center of the can bottoms. Then, from the bottom side, we'd poke one end of the long cord into each hole. We pulled the string out through the cans and tied big knots in the ends. By stretching the cord tight, we could communicate quite well at surprisingly long distances. Each can was both transmitter and receiver. My school chum Katherine and her cousin Henry strung the cord from second floor windows across Maryland Avenue and had a great time communicating!

Imagine finding reference to string telephones in an 1876 encyclopedia telling of experiments done with string phones as early as 1667! Robert Hooke, a German scientist, declared that "the theory of the telephone is simple," and said that string telephones transmitted sound waves <u>mechanically</u>. Two hundred years later a German, Johann Phillips Revs, first transmitted sound waves <u>electrically</u>. His device had both transmitter and receiver and he named it the "telephone." 🚲

"NUMBER PLEASE"

When I was a little girl, children didn't use telephones without permission. Our phone rang a lot but not all calls were for us. On a line with six or eight customers, every phone rang and the whole line was busy when a neighbor was talking. Everyone knew who was being called by the ring signals; ours was one long and two shorts. They knew when the line was cleared because people "rang off" with a short jingle on the party line.

Mom would grind a little handle on the side of the tall oak phone box. A friendly woman called "Central" would ask, "Number, please?" Mom would push a black button as she talked and before giving the number she might say, "We missed you at church Sunday." They'd chat as Central selected Mom's "plug in" to connect her to the other phone on the mutual system.

Eavesdropping might have seemed nosy or malicious but it was more often done to be helpful. Central listened in and was glad to relay news or visit a little before pulling the plug to end a conversation. The phone usually jingled but it roared furiously when there was trouble and others would go and listen in. In 1922 when our house was engulfed in flames, Central rang frantically and screamed, "Meyers's house is on fire," over and over. Our home was a total loss but Les and Joe arrived in time to save some hams and bacon slabs from the smoke house just before the roof collapsed.

When I was about 10 years old, I liked going with Mom when she visited her friend in Hinton who was "Central" on the mutual phone system there. The switchboard was in one corner of her bedroom. She sat where she could see it from her living room. When lights went on she'd go to "plug in" so people could talk to each other.

"Number please," she'd say. Then she'd pull up a plug, and stick it into a hole on a different part of the switchboard. The board was sometimes crisscrossed by lots of wires but they didn't get tangled. When a light went off, she'd pull the plug and a weight underneath plopped it back quickly into its special place. Callers kept ringing while she served refreshments and lines were tied up with calls that needed to be disconnected. How I wished to help her or to be a Central! The next week I created my own switchboard using a board and an orange crate. I whittled 10 or 12 plugs, bored lots of holes in the board and some in the orange crate. I made little sand bags for weights to pull the plugs back into their proper places at the end of my imaginary calls. I was sure that I'd be a Central saying "Number, please," when I grew up! 🚲

MRS. VENABLE'S CHRISTMAS TREE

Mrs. Venable held a large kettle while her "milkman" poured from his big gallon measuring cup. The milk was still foamy and warm from the cow.

"Mr. Meyers," Mrs. Venable said, "Would your little girl like to cut a cedar tree to sell me?"

He nodded and asked how tall it should be.

"Oh, about up to my shoulder," she said. "I'll give her 25 cents, the same as I'd pay at the store."

The year was 1922 and I was that little girl.

I suddenly found myself launched into the business of selling wild cedar trees from the woods on our dairy farm. I still had to rinse milk bottles for 25 cents a week, "plus your keep," as Dad would say.

At eight years of age, I was just old enough to manage an ax. I cut the trees from a hillside south of our house. When it snowed, I hauled the trees on my homemade sled, but when there was no snow, I carried them over my shoulder.

Dad arranged his milk route so he could drop my brother and me off at the University Laboratory School. He then delivered milk, and trees, to our customers' homes.

Why did people want cedar trees for Christmas? Because Boone County has an overabundance of these fragrant, native trees. In those days, nobody dreamed that Christmas trees could be cut months ahead and hauled across the country.

"A big tree crowds the living room," my mom said. "And it takes too many expensive ornaments." Store-bought ornaments were made of very thin glass and we treasured the four or five that we had. It was a major catastrophe when one dropped.

My brother and I would hunt for a cedar tree that had a bird's nest in it – a nice spot for Santa to leave a few coins. We'd make colored paper chains of interlocking circles and instead of candles, we'd use little candy canes. I still remember the taste of those dusty peppermint canes when we ate them on New Year's Eve.

During Christmas tree season, I'd rinse milk bottles and then hurry to the woods, ax in hand, and I'd seldom be back with my trees before it was pitch dark. It was a self-perpetuating enterprise which lasted into my high school years. By then a 25-cent tree brought nearly a dollar.

Some of my old customers moved away and others died, but I sold a few cedars even after entering the University of Missouri. That childhood business influenced the next phase of my life too.

My boyfriend and I were home one day when a regular customer called to order a tree. I was a bit embarrassed for my boyfriend to know about this menial "job" of mine. I was quite favorably impressed, however, when he helped me cut and carry the tree. That boyfriend was my last, because I married him.

Several years later, my husband and I planted Scotch pines

on our own farm. We had Columbia's first "cut-your-own-tree" farm. While not as fragrant as cedar trees, pines are real, not man-made-put-it-together trees that are stored in attics year after year. Our Scotch pines "as high as Mrs. Venable's shoulder" sold for 18 times as much as she paid me for that first tree!

Jim and me in our winter best.

Dad, Mom's brother Lawrence, Jim and me. I was probably fussing because of that bonnet and long sleeves.

KITCHEN WORK
OR FARM WORK?

My brother and I worked right along with our parents because that's the way families were—teams, like our mules, working shoulder to shoulder to pull the load.

We all worked together to have a productive garden, successful crops and a tip-top retail diary operation. Country women took pride in having their washing on the line early in the day, in making neat patches on men's overalls and in providing their families with tasty, nourishing food. I liked helping on the farm more than helping in the kitchen because I enjoyed being outdoors. I think that the main attraction was seeing things growing and changing day by day. Housework needed to be done over and over, always the same, but I helped there too.

Each year, soon after the corn came up, Dad would say, "This will be a good weekend to replant corn." He'd sharpen our hoes and my brother and I would fill our overall pockets with corn. Our job was to put seeds in where the planter had skipped so space wasn't wasted. We'd each work two rows at a time because there weren't too many skipped places. When I found one, I'd turn the hoe sideways to chop a triangular hole

about three inches deep, drop in three kernels and drag dirt
back to fill the hole. As I stepped on the dirt to firm it around
the seed, I knew that three more plants, six more ears, would
grow in that spot. I was doing something worthwhile.

Dad, like many other farmers, used to "check" his corn
rows. That meant that they could cultivate across the width of
the field as well as down the long rows. This left few weeds but
it wasted space. With the development of commercial fertiliz-
ers, farmers began to plant more seeds in each row. That
ended cross cultivation and meant that we would chop weeds
out with hoes. Dad hired a neighbor boy George Williams and
all four of us worked part of the time. We'd work two rows at
a time, as with replanting. I'd look back at the rows where
those weeds were wilting on the ground and be glad they
wouldn't rob the soil of food and water needed for corn plants.

One year, after the corn was laid by and too tall for the
cultivator to pass over without damage, there were still weeds
between the rows. We hitched our "riding mule" to the one-row
garden cultivator. I rode as Dad walked behind, guiding the
cultivator by its two handles. My job was to keep Jack from
stepping on corn and to keep him from snipping tasty leaves.

In geography class that September, when we were studying
farming, our teacher read, "Corn is planted in rows that are 18
inches apart." I flung my hand in the air. "That's wrong!" I
said, "I've been riding a mule between corn rows this summer
and I know he's wider than 18 inches!" The teacher called
Mom that evening and said that I'd been impudent. Mom
agreed that I had, but tactfully verified the fact that corn rows
were farther apart than the width of that mule. 🚲

MOM'S EXPRESSIONLESS FACE

As a preschooler my world was about six miles long and a mile wide. We lived three miles from Columbia's Happy Hollow and three from Olivet Christian Church at the country cross-roads called Harg. My world extended south to the D. D. Moss farm, a woodsy area where we picked blackberries in summer and gathered walnuts and hickory nuts in autumn. That was on the south fork of Grindstone Creek. My boundary to the north, about a mile from where we picked blackberries and nuts, was on Bill Sublett's farm. He was a truck farmer and shared leftover melons on cooling-off evenings. We went to the Flat Rock swimming hole several times a week. It was a deep hole of water in the north fork of Grindstone Creek. That was my first encounter with swimming and with what I thought was going to be a personal tragedy!

Families met to cool off following hot summer days in the hayfield or over the hot wood stove at canning time. We swam in the work clothes we had on and usually went home wet. The water was just barely over Dad's head in its deepest spot and there was a nice sand beach near an outcropping of limestone rocks. Those rocks gave the spot its name of "Flat Rock."

Mom was "deathly afraid of water" but I had no reason to understand what that meant. She and I shared a spot in shallow water because I didn't learn to swim until the next summer when I was six. She taught me how to "mud crawl" with hands on the creek bottom, and she encouraged me saying, "Soon you'll swim well enough to save yourself." That didn't mean much yet either.

One summer evening Uncle Lawrence and Aunt Ethel Henry went with us to the creek to cool off. Uncle Lawrence, Mom's younger brother, was a kidder and he'd come by and talk to Mom, saying, "It's easy, Nancy. I can teach you to swim."

But no! She didn't budge. Later I was nearby when he approached her with his face in the water. Suddenly he looked up and grabbed Mom's feet as if to pull her in. Mom's eyes rolled back in their sockets and she went limp. "Scared to death!" I thought! Lawrence and Dad and others helped pull her up on the beach.

"Nancy! Speak to me," Dad pleaded as we massaged her arms and legs and lifted her heavy head with closed eyes. It seemed an eternity—those few minutes before she regained consciousness. I never forgot the look of her horrible, expressionless face!

Of course she was all right and Uncle Lawrence was sorry. He said over and over, "Sis, I was just kidding. I didn't mean any harm. Please forgive me." She promised her forgiveness but she certainly never forgot. 🚲

TEACHER/WIFE/MOTHER

CHUB'S UNDERWATER LIGHTS

In 1941, the Columbia Daily Tribune stated,

"The 6th annual water carnival will be presented tonight in the Christian College swimming pool under the direction of Mrs. Sue Gerard. The theme, which takes place at the bottom of the ocean, is built around the dream of a little boy who falls asleep and dreams that he's in the center of a court of mermaids.

"The carnival will include a special underwater swimming number with novelty lighting effects, designed and constructed by W. F. Gerard. The soloist will present a spectacular effect with strokes, surface diving, underwater swimming and performing various water ballet stunts."

This "novelty lighting effect" was a set of 16 flashlight bulbs, powered by four flashlight batteries and worn by a swimmer in a darkened pool room. I first learned that underwater lights could be used safely in the mid 1930s. An American Red Cross Field Representative from Iowa told me how it could be done. My boyfriend Chub Gerard, an electrical engineering student at MU, assured me that four flashlight batteries could not possibly be dangerous in the water. After we married, he designed and made Christian College's first set of underwater lights.

He strapped four size D flashlight batteries together and secured them to a belt. The battery pack was worn on the swimmer's back. Four small wires carried power to 16 flashlight bulbs on arms and legs. We tied those wires in place with elastic tapes. Chub said tiny switches could rust or malfunction; instead, the swimmer would just twist two bare wires together to illuminate the bulbs.

A student in my Water Carnival Class volunteered to do the solo, and I helped her work out a routine for what we called "water ballet." She had practiced with the wires and batteries in place, but we hadn't practiced with lights illuminated lest we'd drain too much power from the batteries. On show night, when the pool area began to fill with spectators, the soloist said, "I can't do it. I'm simply afraid!" It was the thought of twisting those two bare wires together that cinched the thing.

I wasn't giving up. "O.K., gals," I said, "tie these wires on me. I'm not afraid." I knew the music well and it was no problem to include the stunts we had chosen for her routine. I just swam hither and yon to the familiar music, but it was certainly not synchronized. It was a beautiful thing to see the lights almost disappear into deep water and then come shooting back up as I pushed from the pool bottom. I swam everything I could think of: back strokes, breast stroke, crawl, surface dives, rolling from back crawl to front crawl, somersaults and rolls, much splashing at times when I was up, catching my breath. When the music ended I untwisted those bare wires, climbed out at the shallow end of the pool and disappeared behind the shower stalls while the applause roared.

There was never any doubt after that about the safety of underwater lights. Chub had said, "It's no more dangerous than carrying a metal flashlight in the rain." We used his set of lights for several years, replacing batteries for each show. When we were planning a show later, someone asked, "Why don't we have a duet with the underwater lights?" Great idea!

Maurice Wightman, Christian College's wonderfully creative man who could do everything, made four new sets, improving on the original set. By 1972 when I retired, Maurice had made enough lights for our routines to have eight swimmers. For about 20 water shows, Chub's "invention" was the highlight of our performances.

Christian College swimmers wearing underwater lights.

UNCLE ARCHIE

Uncle Archie Gerard came for a week's visit and he stayed four years. He was a great storyteller, he loved a mid-morning cigar and he almost never missed going to a Kentucky Derby. He often quoted the Bible and told a dirty story in the same conversation. Being with us on the farm brought him memories of the happiest days of his life when he and Edie and their two children lived on a farm in Pike County, Illinois.

Aunt Edie, his beloved wife, died before her 30th birthday leaving Unc with a little girl and boy. He lived more than 90 years and never loved any other woman. Edie was in Heaven and he'd see her again, but it puzzled him that she died as a beautiful young woman and he'd meet her as a wrinkled, deaf old man. It also puzzled him that Russia sent a "sputnik" out into who-knows-where. Was his Edie O.K. out there?

Our Nancy and Walt were early elementary school age when Unc became very important in their lives. Unc read "The Little Engine That Could" and "Little Black Sambo" to them so often that he'd make up extra incidents to break the monotony.

"Unc," Walt would say, "get your glasses!"

A WAR TIME CHRISTMAS SURPRISE

We were living in a tiny two-room apartment at the time of our second WW II Christmas. Chub was a Coast Guardsman assigned to teach at General Motors Institute of Technology. He taught enlisted men and officers to operate and repair the Gray Marine Diesel engine used to power landing craft and other vessels.

We rented an apartment in the home of an elderly couple. It was a cozy upstairs apartment with a west porch, nice on summer evenings. I was teaching at the YWCA that December.

We put up a little artificial tree that I had carried on the bus the year before to New York City. Decorating it required about 15 minutes or less. Since we'd been married six years, we were quite aware of each other's cherished, family holiday traditions. The Meyers family celebrated on December 24th because of Dad's milking schedule. We always had a freshly cut cedar from our woods.

The Gerard family saved everything until Christmas morning. Gifts that came in the mail went unopened and Santa's presents were in hiding. Chub and his five sisters were permitted to get up early on Christmas morning and peek into the room where Santa had been, but they were not allowed to enter before all ate a good nourishing breakfast. Then the fun began.

We knew, on our lonely Christmas in Flint, that his sister Louise would remember us. She was my kind of giver, hand-embroidered pillow cases, towels edged with elaborate tatting and other unique things like that. After we were in bed one night, Chub said, "Louise's package came today." I asked about it because it wasn't under the tree. "I hid it," he said. "We're not opening it until Christmas morning."

After a few moments I begged, "Couldn't we just put it out to help decorate that sickly little tree?" He was still adamant about saving it till Christmas morning, which was several days away. "Where did you hide it?" I asked.

"Under this bed," he answered.

I reminded him of the time that Gram Willingham had mailed us a shoe box full of fresh broccoli from her garden. It was wrapped in damp paper towels and wax paper and arrived in perfect condition.

Finally he agreed that we could take off the brown paper and put the gift out to liven up the room with the colored wrapping. We got out of bed and opened the gift. There was no holiday paper! There was, instead, a wonderful freshly dressed hen!

I won that one! ᴋ🐔ʟ

WE DID WHAT WE COULD WITH WHAT WE HAD

Columbia's 1935 experiment in supervised playgrounds was so successful that money was available for more equipment, supplies and a full program the following summer. Local persons experienced in crafts, athletics and children's activities of various kinds were chosen as leaders, regardless of whether they were trained for the job. I had completed a university class called "Plays and Games" and was assigned as one of two leaders on Grant School's playground.

We had been taught that playgrounds were fenced, that participants were enrolled by age groups, that adequate funds were available and that play areas would be level and well marked for various sports and games. Not so at Eugene Field School, or Douglas, Grant or Ridgeway. We learned to conserve, to improvise and to use volunteer help. We did, as Theodore Roosevelt advised: "Do what you can, with what you have, where you are."

Grant's playground space was limited, thermometers climbed to new heights and the dust was almost unbearable. That was in 1936 and we had a summer of quiet activities. One special event was a pet show with a motley array of animals, most of whom had never before been on a leash or dressed in costume. We got along fine.

The next summer I was assistant director, helping Johnny Cooper who was one of MU's all time great athletes. He was chosen to coach at a high school away from central Missouri and had to report for duty a few weeks before the end of the summer program. I was in charge of the four playgrounds, with no assistant, for the last few weeks.

The next summer I had the top job and my assistant was principal of one of the schools on which we had a playground. It wasn't easy telling a school principal what to do and when to do it because it was more important to maintain a good future relationship between the city and the public school system. He stayed close to his office, except for special events such as inter-playground ball games and occasional visits to other playgrounds. He'd stand tall with arms folded and sometimes adjust his straw sailor hat, tap it in place and turn and leave. "Just let them play on their own" was his philosophy.

I could have used that fellow's prestige and his help on one occasion. I had arrived on a playground to find things unusually quiet. The two leaders were talking together and the big boys were under a shade tree whispering. The rest of the children were in the sand pile or jumping rope, paying no attention to the tension between the leaders and the boys. I soon learned that one troublesome boy had pulled a long knife, threatening my female leader. With courage I didn't know I had, I eyeballed the fellow, strode across the playground straight to him and said, "Give me that knife!" To my surprise, he did! That was the only scary moment of the summer.

Dating was different in the thirties!

Me, in foreground, in charge of classes at Columbia's Water and Light Plant pool.

MRS. ROOSEVELT
AND TEEN TOWN

I had part-time jobs with Parks and Recreation several times after there was a full time director. One summer when W.C. Harris managed the huge Water and Light Plant swimming pool, he asked me to be his assistant. My job was to plan and teach free classes and to do public water safety demonstrations. It was a fun summer for me. I taught Red Cross Life Saving and swimming for beginners and others, including some water ballet. With the philosophy of "If you entertain people hugely, you can educate them gently at the same time," we put on a full-blown water show at the end of the summer.

We also scheduled an evening class for "adults who think they can't be taught to swim." Several who enrolled were more than 80 years old. Two women about my age said if I taught them to swim across the pool by the end of the summer, they'd take me out to supper and a show. They swam the 85 feet, in shallow water using resting back stroke. They paid off and we became good friends for life.

During WW II the Parks and Recreation Department received national publicity. W.C. Harris had arranged for young people to have an after school gathering place in the basement of the old, vacant Methodist Church which faced Broadway at Short Street. Teens themselves renovated the area and, with recreation leaders, scheduled fun activities for after school and weekends. They offered $5 for the teen who suggested the best name for their gathering place. "Teen Town" was the winner.

By coincidence Teen Town was in full swing the day that Mrs. Eleanor Roosevelt visited Columbia. She was fascinated by the do-it-yourself accomplishments and the positive effect it had on young people. She told about it in her daily syndicated column, "My Day." Letters poured in to the recreation office requesting details about this project. I worked part-time, preparing a brochure to answer those many inquiries. Later, it became necessary to move Teen Town across the street to a three floor brick building east of Central Dairy and west of the First Baptist Church. A young couple named Williams were the leaders. The city asked Christian College's president to allow me to add another responsibility to my teaching job. It was agreed and I helped the Williams's beg and repair furniture, make ping pong tables, paint walls, get pop machines, libraries and juke boxes. Thanks to Eleanor Roosevelt and her unscheduled visit, "Teen Towns" like ours dotted the nation at a time when recreation on the home front was of utmost importance.

A DEER AT DAWN
CHANGED OUR PLANS

When we bought a worn out farm for less than $30 per acre, the county road was not always passable, the one room dwelling had no dependable water supply and the "bath" was at the end of a path. The REA electric line was available, but mail and telephone service were about two miles away. My retired father, O.D. Meyers, advised and helped Chub build terraces, fertilize the soil and get the first crop in. Our two toddlers and I took lunch for the men and spent the afternoons at the farm.

Dad surprised Chub and me by giving us ten registered shorthorn cows from his herd. Our first corn crop came up and looked great until it was about waist high. Like other farmers in the Midwest, we watched the sky for clouds that never came. The corn leaves began to rustle in the hot wind and we knew that this crop would not produce grain. It was soon obvious that, if we were to have feed for those ten cows, we'd have to make silage out of this failed crop. There was no silo but we heard that some farmers were putting chopped corn into earthen pits. Chub chose one of the remaining deep ditches and called for a bulldozer to make us a pit silo.

Chopped corn stalks and leaves made enough silage to take the ten cows through the winter and, as farmers do, we determined to have that bumper crop the next year. We also decided to close our home and spend the next summer at the farm.

I started a little garden in front of the farm house but the corn fields almost surrounded the dwelling. We made Walt and Nancy a tractor tire sand pile, hung a bag swing from a limb of the mulberry tree and installed a jungle gym.

Early one morning that summer, I was admiring our tall green corn from the outdoor "John" when I heard a neighbor's rooster crowing and a gobbler calling to a wild turkey hen. The sky was deep blue with cotton ball clouds. Suddenly I saw a deer in our yard and we stared at each other, unafraid! That moment changed my outlook on life. The deer was standing in our yard as if he owned the place—and he did, of course!

Here we had 160 acres of fresh air and space—great for raising children. Chub and I knew we couldn't make a living on such a small acreage, but we decided we could both work in town and could increase the herd to support the country life we wanted for Nancy and Walt. That winter an architect helped us plan to modernize and enlarge the farm house. The next spring, we rented our home near town and went to the farm to stay. Relatives and many friends helped us build.

Chub was elected to the school board and I helped the Turner School get its first telephone before Nancy was old enough for first grade. I returned to Christian College to teach water sports and recreation and Chub became an inspector of new construction at the University of Missouri. We installed our own water system, helped clear the roadsides so a school bus could get through and needled the county court for a graveled, well maintained road.

It was inconvenient being without a telephone for the next few years, but a space finally became available on a ten-party line—and we loved it here. What a great decision that deer helped us make!

Eva Coleman fitting halos.

GREAT TEACHERS ARE ALIVE IN ALL OF US

To tell the story of two great country school teachers, one white and the other black, is to tell the story of wonderful teachers everywhere. Lucy Douglas and Eva Coleman worked together to integrate black and white children into one new school called Reorganized II, or "R-II," for short. Our school successfully combined five all-white schools with "Grindstone Colored" before integration was required by law. When *Ebony* magazine's editor spoke at the University of Missouri, I proposed an article, "I'm Glad My Daughter's Teacher is a Negro." He snapped at the opportunity saying, "I'll pay well for that!" When *Ebony* received my manuscript, they sent a Chicago photographer for three days to take photos of Eva Coleman's third grade classroom and of Nancy and her good friend Betty Ann Williams in the cafeteria, on the playground and riding in the school bus. *Ebony* used 11 pictures with the story.

Why all of this interest in the fact that Nancy's third grade teacher was black?

For the first time in Missouri, children of two races were learning together, playing together and eating together at school.

Our rural school board courageously brought six one-room elementary schools, and their teachers, together in a new modern building. The six teachers previously taught all grades in one-room schools.

Lucy Douglas had taught eight grades, about 25 pupils, at Turner School for white children. Eva Coleman had taught even more at a crowded one-room school named "Grindstone Colored." Some of her pupils walked more than two miles each way carrying their lunch boxes.

Mrs. Douglas was chosen as principal of the new school and Eva Coleman taught third grade. Behind the scenes they worked together to help all of the children know and respect each other regardless of color. They worked through the PTA to help parents do the same thing. They solved problems quietly as they arose and when there were difficult times, these two gentle women performed miracles.

Few children had attended a school which had a gymnasium, hot lunches, a large playground or bus transportation. One school had a telephone and an indoor toilet, thanks to the Parent-Teachers' Association. Pupils eagerly accepted these improvements, but there were social adjustments to be made. When pupils were divided into classes by age, all classes were mixed-race classes. Only a few black third graders got to be with their beloved Mrs. Coleman. Most children had to accept new teachers and strangers for classmates.

All of the teachers greeted their former students with just the right amount of attention in the cafeteria, hallways and on the playground, but it was the planning and leadership of Lucy Douglas and Eva Coleman that made this experiment in integration work smoothly. Soon all of the students looked to these two women for guidance. Parents hid their apprehension, for the most part, and several volunteered regularly to help make this new educational system a success.

I had a two-hour lunch break at the college. Knowing that some of the children's favorite games were not appropriate for a newly integrated playground, I went out to R-II and supervised the noon recess for several weeks. By avoiding games like Red Rover, Farmer in the Dell and "choosing up side" games, we helped the children get acquainted. Nonselective activities included rope jumping, track events and singing games. After a few weeks, prejudice seldom surfaced on the playground.

Practicing for the Christmas play, a child asked, "Mrs. Douglas, do you really think that's right?"

"What, honey?"

"That the mother and father in the play have both black and white children?" Truly surprised, Mrs. Douglas and Mrs. Coleman looked at each other and laughed. Then everybody laughed and went on with the practice—with black and white angels and black and white snowmen!

Those two wonderful women succeeded in teaching the children that it's normal for people of different races to work together, laugh together and learn together. That was in 1958 and it was a new idea in education.

When Lucy Douglas was approaching her 90th birthday, we spoke at length about those early days of integrating the school now called New Haven. Lucy said, "You know, Sue, if we had it all to do over again, I'd do it just the same."

"Yes," I agreed, "because you did it right in 1958!"

UNC'S BIG BALL
OF WORMS

Fishing worms are everywhere in April, nowhere in August. This is April.

Uncle Archie took his cane and pushed a small plank over this morning and discovered the fattest fishing worms an angler could dream of finding.

He called and both kids and I went running with three tin cans and a potato digging fork. In about ten minutes we had picked up and counted 140 worms. Put the ball of bait together and we'd have had a ball of pure worms as big as a croquet ball.

Nancy and Walt filled the cans with dirt and set them in the cool moist fruit cellar to be used this weekend. Wonder if catching fish will be as exciting as collecting this big batch of worms?

THE ANTICS OF LONE WHITE ROOSTER

My good friend Helen Vemer told me about the white rooster that someone gave her and I was surprised when she said, "Sue, I want to give you this beautiful white rooster."

I asked why, but for the life of me, I can't remember what she said. Looking back, I think they couldn't face the thought of making chicken soup out of this beautiful fellow. And then again, perhaps he was about to drive the Vemers out of their minds, as he did us later.

We put him in a gunny sack and brought him home, more as a favor to Helen than from any desire to have a rooster. We didn't have chickens or any fenced place in which to keep him. In only a short time, he was eating his crushed corn and also drinking some of the cats' milk. The mother cat didn't mind because Chub was giving them an ample supply of Skyline's warm foamy milk, twice a day.

Lone Rooster had a beautiful voice and was proud of it. He'd stretch up tall, rare back and sing out "Got the Whole Wor-old," in the proper timing and in true tone. He actually did have his "whole world in his hand." For one thing, he was part-time sitter for the kittens. If they started to climb out of their cardboard box, he'd gently peck on the back of their heads to make them stay in. He paid little attention to them except when their mother was away. She had probably clawed his face to prevent his meddling ways.

Lone Rooster could be counted on to crow his "got the whole world" at about any time of day or early morning. We didn't need an alarm because his song woke us in time to get to school and work. He had no respect, however, for our wanting to sleep late on Saturdays and Sundays.

Occasionally Lone Rooster nudged Fuey, our Pekingese dog, as if to initiate a romp or a fight. Fuey would turn his face away in disgust and then crawl underneath the lawn mower where the rooster couldn't reach him. The little dog would chase stray dogs away or make the barn cats scamper up the mulberry tree, but he was smart enough to keep a safe distance from that big rooster. He had probably felt the sting of its spurs.

When Lone Rooster discovered that the family ate breakfast near a low picture window, he joined us almost every morning. I'd knocked on the window to make him quit scratching in the flower beds and he'd disappear—and then come right back. He narrowly missed the soup kettle the day he scratched my seeds out of the dry ground, piled them in a dusty mound and then sat and squirmed back and forth, dusting his feathers.

The kittens grew and ignored Lone Rooster. Lonely, he suddenly discovered the image of a white rooster reflected in the glass of our utility room's storm door. At last he had found a companion! He went through his repertoire of antics to attract and impress this potential friend. Getting no response from the "intruder," he flapped his wings wildly and jumped high in the air, trying to peck his reflection's head. I often chased him away lest he break the glass. This performance was repeated occasionally when the light was just right.

Our lone white rooster with his bright red comb died a natural death one summer when we were away, but we will never forget him.

When Lone White Rooster crowed he sang, "Got the whole wor-ald."

"NANCY"
HALF A YEAR OLD

Pablum on your forehead,
Pablum on your chin.
Pablum on your mother
And on the chair she's in.
Pablum to the north of you,
Pablum to the south.
Wonder if some Pablum
Found its way into your mouth?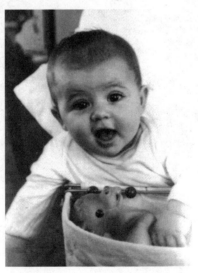

SHIPPING LLOYD'S CATTLE

It's 17 degrees below zero, a cattle truck is stuck in a drift on our road and the only two tractors within miles are on the wrong side of the truck with no way to get around it. From my warm, sunny window I see steam and snow blowing straight across country from the truck, the tractors and the men as they wrestle with tow chains. Our dog Misty and Willis's dog, Brownie, had a scrap in the backyard while Willis and Chub were trying to decide what to do about the cattle truck. Now the dogs are romping like the best of buddies as they watch the men and machines battle a record cold winter problem.

It all started several days ago when Lloyd Bennett's cattle got through a fence and into the bales of hay that were to last them all winter. "All winter" has already been about a year it seems. But Lloyd, in his upper 70s, and his wife Velma wore themselves out trying to get the cattle out of the hay. Lloyd breathed too much frigid air and is not well at all. The cattle were still in with the hay when the snows came. The drifts got so deep that Velma couldn't tell if they were still eating. Cows have a way of messing up the hay by sleeping on it and scatter-

ing it. That could mean the end of a winter's supply. Willis
discovered this predicament when he went by tractor to take
Bennett's their mail. Their driveway was drifted shut. It still
is. A few days later, Velma called and asked if we had a loading
chute as they would have to ship their 12 cows and the bull to
the St. Louis market.

I look out the window again and finally see the tractors
pulling the cattle truck. They're like a procession. Willis's
tractor is tied to Chub's tractor which is still tied to the huge
empty cattle truck. The playful dogs are leading the way, of
course.

Yesterday Walt, Willis's sons and two of Velma's nephews
came to help the men round up the cattle and drive them over
here. It was all they could do, cows and men, to plow through
the drifts with none of the usual breakaways. It was a long,
tiring walk of almost a mile.

They put the 13 animals into our corral. This morning there
were 14! Mother Nature seems to choose the very worst time
to deliver babies. This was one of those times. What to do?
The baby calf wouldn't survive the trip to St. Louis in the
crowded truck and we don't have enough hay to feed one more
cow, that's for sure. The weather prediction is for another
month of this!

I'll have another cup of tea because the story isn't ended yet.
Part of yesterday's work was to scrape and scoop drifts away
from the loading chute. Our backyard is a labyrinth of snow
ridges and when I went out yesterday to the pottery, I thought
I wasn't going to get back.

Shipping all of their cattle is a traumatic experience for
Lloyd and Velma. They've been the best about taking care of

people who needed help, all of these years. They've lived a self-sufficient farm life for over 50 years. They have a cellar full of canned everything: fruit, vegetables, meats, everything! But the Bennett's must be restless today, sitting by the fire, while the neighbors stomp through bitter cold and snow to rescue their cattle.

I check the window one more time. They must have the cattle loaded as the procession has started again, this time in reverse. Willis and tractor, Chub and tractor are all chained to the cattle truck. They slowly move down the hill, over the crossing, and now up the hill. Yes! They made it with that heavy load. Brownie leads the way and Misty is bringing up the rear. She leaps across the snow piled at the roadside and then crawls under the fence for a few laps around the pasture.

Oh no! It's all come to a halt at about the place where the truck first got stuck. Willis's chain must have broken as the men are working on the hitch between the tractors. What if that loaded truck is there for keeps?

Now it's moving again, thank goodness. The big stock rack is flopping side-to-side a bit as they pull it out of the drift. They're stopped at the entrance to the driveway, hopefully to unhitch and let the truck take it from there.

The parade is over. The tractors are unhitched and the truck is moving slowly out of sight. Willis and Chub must be frozen! Two tractors, two men, two dogs, are coming this way, grading the drive as they proceed. Misty has rolled in the snow and is absolutely white. Brownie has better sense. Dogs love snow, but men do not!

I guess the ordeal is over. I'm pretty useless as I sit and watch, but I do have their coffee water hot.

BEES WERE
MAKING HONEY
IN OUR KITCHEN

One morning when our children were getting ready for Sunday school, I called, "Hey, kids, come see what's going on in the glass bee hive." Nancy and Walt stood on stools to see two "feelers" coming out of a tiny hole in the center of one cell. The rest of the bees went on with their work, unconcerned. We craned our necks to see a bee trying to chew her way out of the six-sided wax cell. We knew it was a worker bee because the cells for drones are much larger and have unusual shapes. There are few drone cells and thousands of worker cells in a successful colony.

In an incredible division of labor, some worker bees are housekeepers and nurses. They clean and prepare a cell before the queen arrives to put an egg in it. She inspects it briefly, head foremost, and then backs out and turns around to enter in reverse. She quickly lays an egg, attaching it to the center of the hexagon cell's rear wall. Then off she goes to the next cleaned cell. She sometimes lays 1500 eggs in a single day. Unbelievably, she can lay a fertile egg in a proper cell and an infertile egg in a sagging or misshapen cell.

The queen does not groom herself or feed herself or choose the place for laying the next egg! Worker bees take care of her and they even "hand feed" the queen. She is not a queen in the sense of being a ruler. She is an efficient egg laying machine and that's about all.

Back to that egg: worker bees put just the right amount of the right kind of food in with the egg and then cap it with wax and walk away. When the egg hatches, the larva feeds on royal jelly till its supply is gone. It will eat a mixture of "bee bread" and honey after that and will not mature enough to reproduce. This controlled diet stops the insect's development at what we might call adolescence. Although the workers are all female, it's most unusual that one could ever lay an egg. The larva, with head turned toward the cell's cap, grows till hatching time. This was happening hundreds of times in our kitchen!

Having a glass-sided hive on a tall shelf in the kitchen cabinet was another one of my "wild ideas." This observation hive has only one frame, whereas production hives have 10 in each section of the colony's hive. I bored a hole in the wooden window frame and used a chemist's large glass tube to join the hive to the window frame hole so bees could come and go to gather pollen, nectar and water.

I used strips of annealed copper, secured by duct tape, to make the glass passage way "bee tight." I couldn't risk their getting loose in the house. A wooden block, tacked to the outside of the window frame, provided a necessary landing board for their coming and going. By opening a hive in our apiary of 21 colonies, I selected one frame to put in the kitchen. It had to be one which included everything, except the queen, that a colony needs for survival: honey, unhatched brood, open cells with workers fanning their wings to evaporate water from the nectar, cells of "bee bread" for food and open cells in which I could see an egg attached inside. The eggs, or larvae less than four days old, were necessary because this colony would die without a queen and I didn't dare have the colony's queen on the frame I removed from an active hive. In the new location, the workers would know immediately that they were queenless, and within a few days they'd be raising a queen for themselves!

We kept the doors on the glass hive for several days to allow them to become adjusted to new surroundings. Then I opened the exit/entry hole and within a short time we watched worker bees walking in a spiral, examining this unusual entrance to their small hive and making their way to the outside. Some took new jobs. For example, I had not likely brought any guard bees, but soon there were guards flying around outside to protect the entrance.

My sink was full of dishes to be washed, but that didn't matter. I stayed there watching till I saw bees going straight out of the tube and wobbling as they walked back in, laden with pollen in their rear leg baskets. Hooray! My crazy idea was working!

That Sunday morning we watched the "feelers" extend out of the little hole in the cell and then disappear over and over again. Progress was slow but the insect inside was obviously chewing to make the hole large enough for its shoulders and body to emerge.

"Let's close their exit," Walt said. "Then we can set it where we can all see without taking turns on this stool."

Good idea. We put it on the dining table and about an hour

later the little head was coming through the hole, but the shoulders were much too big.

That wiped out our plans for Sunday school! Chub joined the vigil and the bee kept chewing. Finally she forced her way through the hole and stretched and groomed herself with her front legs. Then without eating or getting instructions from other workers, she made a "bee line," stepping on many other workers as she went to a particular cell. She immediately began housekeeping chores as her hundreds of sisters had done on their first day after hatching. How did the newly emerged bee know? Who told her which cell was waiting for her cleaning services? Wasn't she hungry after all that work of chewing out? Would she even get to groom the queen or guard the hive or carry supplies from blossoms? According to Murray Hoyt, in his "World of Bees" (Bonanza, NY), there's no head of the colony, no foremen, no subordinates.

We soon lost sight of her in the mob and our show was over! Sunday school and church were over too! 🐝

WHERE'S THE BUS?

Friday afternoon the school bus didn't come at the usual time. We waited. Then we called the neighbors. Other kids were home and ours were not. Chub went in the car to look for them. No luck.

Margaret Klug's children were home and they told us that the regular bus had a flat and they brought a replacement. Our Nancy and Walt got on that second bus. A half hour passed.

I called the bus company. A man who answered said all of the busses were in and the drivers had gone home. "Everybody's gone home but me." The manager? He lives in Fayette. I don't know how to call him." Surely there was some way to reach that man. "You just call back the first thing Monday morning and he'll be here."

"Monday! Mister, these are my children!" I shouted.

We got back in the car. The Powell's children told us that Nancy and Walt had volunteered to walk the half mile from our mailbox corner to help the driver get back to the lot on time. "They started walking..." We were getting closer.

How could they have been lost in the 1 1/2 miles to our

house from Rangeline Road?

We found them at Velma and Lloyd's house. I hadn't called the Bennett's because they had no children and their house was not within sight of the lane. Our Nancy and Walt loved the Bennetts, though. The kids had detoured halfway down our lane and dropped in for a visit!

A DIFFERENT EASTER DINNER

As we left Olivet Church on Easter Sunday in 1961, we saw black smoke in the direction of our farm four miles away. We took an Easter lily to Chub's mother in Columbia and she met us saying, "You have a phone call." It was our friend, Petie Davison, saying, "Your house is OK, but the shed is on fire and several firemen are here and others are coming up the driveway."

I had cooked a whole ham for Easter – planning to freeze some later, but by 3 p.m. I was begging my guests to eat more ham. My guests were 14 <u>volunteer</u> firemen in white shirts, suit pants and their best shoes – dirty and tired but happy. They had saved our home and its contents. In their Easter best, they had pumped water from our small lake, lowering its level by four inches!

Petie said that when they sprayed the back of the house, it steamed! I stepped it off. The elevated gas tank was only 20 stride-steps from the corner of our freezer room, but it didn't ignite. It was full, which had offered more protection than having space above the gas the firemen said. We lost the shed, hay, lawn and garden tools, a beautiful antique sleigh and lots more. The fire was caused by a wind change that fanned a spark where trash had been burned early that morning.

Two things saved our home and everything in it. Our six-year-old neighbor boy named Monte Gibson, who lived a quarter of a mile away, alerted his parents by saying, "There's something wrong over at Gerard's." The adults were shoeing horses that day and didn't get Monte's message at first. He insisted, "There is something wrong!" His mother dashed to the house and called the volunteer firemen. The men got the radio message on their way home from church and headed to our farm.

When dedicated fire fighters, paid or volunteer, need more equipment or training or anything, I always think of those dirty, exhausted men who came in their Sunday best and shared our unusual Easter dinner.

COW BONES

The kids came in the front door shouting, "Mother, we've made a discovery!" They were carrying some of the bony remains of a cow. Nine-year-old Nancy carried the skull with upper jaw and Walt had the lower jaw with most of the teeth intact. They had some other miscellaneous parts as well. All was deposited on the living room floor.

"There's a lot more down in the woods, we can get you all the bones you want," they said. Thanks. I have all of the old cow bones I want. And in spite of the dirt, dead spiders and grass that were falling out, we sat down together to examine the bones of a dead cow—probably one who fell through the ice two years ago. The kids had found the thicket where Chub disposed of carcasses.

We fitted the jaws into their sockets and did the motions a cow would use to nip off grass, to chew her cud and to just rest her jaws. Nancy wanted to see the whole tooth, roots and all, so we pried with a can opener and pulled with some sharp-nosed pliers until a whole tooth came out. Nancy took the tooth and disappeared.

"The neck bones look like a gigantic chicken neck," Walt said, adding "there are a lot of these left in the woods." Gradually we inspected the sinuses, the brain cavity, the place where the lower jaw fit neatly into the depression in the upper part of the skull and I identified the wide flat shoulder blade, which Walt had thought didn't exactly fit in the skeleton of a cow.

Nancy returned with her own dripping toothbrush and a beautiful white tooth from that long-gone cow; the child had scrubbed it with paste on her own toothbrush!

We had a lesson in comparative anatomy and a reminder that learning is exciting and fun. Nancy strung a cord through the eye sockets of the main skull and hung it on the wall above her bed—an eerie sight on moonlit nights when the room was otherwise dark.

Finally they gathered up the bones and I didn't mention the rest of the mess on the rug because they dashed off saying, "Come down there and we'll show you where you can get all the bones you want." Thanks!

A SNOWY
NEW YEAR'S EVE PARTY
IN 1958

The roads all over this part of the country were snow and ice packed; our good friends Guy and Zee Bass couldn't drive from Springfield for their New Year's visit. Nancy, 8, and Walt, 6, were crushed. Chub suggested that we drown our sorrows in a Pepsi and some leftover Christmas candy.

"Let's have our own New Year's party," Nancy whispered as we cleared away the supper dishes. I approved. She pulled Walt into her room and began outlining the party plans. Soon they brought decorated paper hats for us all, and they gave us each a paper cup for popcorn. There was to be a floor show right in our living room.

Nancy wore a sign saying "Song Leder," and was dressed in high heel pumps and the bathroom curtain. Underneath were bright red shorts. She wore her garb as if it were a mink stole. Walt announced that there would be a cover charge of two cents for parent-patrons.

Songs for the floor show were original words to the tunes of "Happy Birthday" and "Jesus Loves Me." Following the music, there was a drawing and Nancy announced that I'd been selected to sing, "I Wisth I Were A Little Fith, I'd Thwim and Thwim in The Deep Blue Thea." As I finished the third verse, they announced that Chub was next. He jumped right up singing "Old Miss Simmon went a swimmin'." The kids stopped him before the chorus because they'd heard him sing it many times and they couldn't wait to get on with their own performing.

Nancy passed the popcorn and both kids left the room. Shortly Walt returned dressed—rather, undressed—as the New Year's baby, his only garment being a bath towel diaper. He served brown "champagne," from a Pepsi bottle wrapped in a dish towel. He popped the cork and then poured the contents into my best crystal sherbet stemware.

At one minute till 9 p.m., we toasted each other with "Auld Lang Syne," singing the only words we could remember, over and over again. A short game of scrabble to celebrate 1959, and the kids were off to bed. We'll repeat the floor show as soon as Guy and Zee can come for their belated visit.

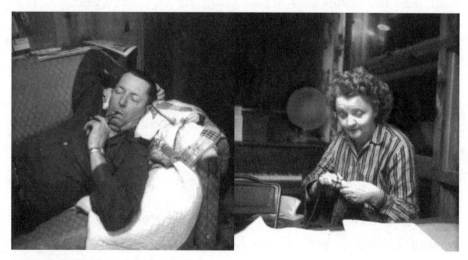

"Uncle" Guy and "Aunt" Zee.

OLD GRAND DAD

Nancy and Walt got off the school bus and were usually home about an hour before I made it home. After teaching until five o'clock, I'd change from bathing suit into street clothes, make some notes to use at the next meeting of each class, lock the pool doors and drive to our farm about 12 miles away. On this day, freezing rain accumulated and tree limbs hung low over our lane. It was beautiful, but the icy road was treacherous. I turned in the driveway and remembered that supper was almost ready in my automatic oven.

The wonderful aroma of beef roast with vegetables was indeed a joy. Nancy and Walt had set the table and we four were soon enjoying our meal. Suddenly Chub blurted out, "Guess what's in the den?" We all jumped up to go see.

My den was a tiny room next to Nancy's bedroom. Shelves of books lined two walls and it had a metal typewriter table, a folding chair and a filing cabinet. What else was in the den this night?

There were gunny sacks on the bare floor and a heap under an old blanket on the sacks. Nancy lifted the corner of the blanket and screamed, "A frozen calf!"

A young heifer had dropped her first calf on the ground and when the storm came, she likely moved to shelter with the rest of the herd. Rain fell and froze an ice crust on her curled-up newborn calf. Chub found it and knew its only hope of survival was to be thawed out and that couldn't happen in an unheated shed. He removed the things on the floor of the den and made a gunny sack nest.

We went back to finish our supper and discuss the calf's chances for life. "We'll drench it as soon as it can swallow," Chub said. Before bedtime I poured a little Old Grand Dad whiskey into a bottle with a long slender neck. Chub held the calf's mouth open while I poked the bottle as far down as possible. We spilled part of the whiskey, but stroked the animal's throat to make him swallow several times.

"Should we take it to the shed for the night?" I asked. Walt and Nancy immediately voted, "No!" We fixed a barricade at the open door so that he couldn't get out of the den.

About midnight, a bump, bump, bumping woke Nancy and she got the rest of us out of bed. The Old Grand Dad whiskey had taken effect and the calf was up on wobbly legs. He had his head caught under the typewriter table. We rescued him, put down more gunny sacks, drenched him with a little more whiskey and went back to bed. The newborn calf looked good the next morning, but his young mother would have nothing to do with him. Luckily, Chub coaxed another mother cow into adopting the miraculous baby. He went through life with the name Old Grand Dad.

OUR SHOVEL
NAMED "BUSTER"

Walt, Nancy and I were rolling big snowballs and decided to make a dinosaur instead of just a snowman. We'd piled up a lot of snow, but Nancy and I visualized "Buster" as being a big guy with long tail, skinny neck and tiny head so we said, "More snow, Walt."

When Walt's inner clock said, "Time for Huckleberry Hound on TV," he looked at Buster and said, "It doesn't look like a dinosaur, it looks like a big pile of snow." Away he went to the tube.

Nancy and I piled and patted and pounded until we had quite a big body. The snow never worked better and the forecast was for a sharp drop to zero or below for that night.

"What'll we do for the neck?" we asked each other. Somebody remembered the long-handled shovel; so we stuck it in place and hung Buster's head from the shovel part, packing and pounding the snow in place. The tail was easy and we made it stick way out behind, on the ground.

By then it looked like a dinosaur, even to Walt. Out he came bragging about "our dinosaur." We had just barely finished the tail and given Buster eyes when the temperature dropped. I got the hose from behind the house and stretched it as far as it would reach. When it got to about 10 degrees, I sprayed the front side of Buster until he froze into solid ice. There wasn't enough hose to spray the back side, so it went un-iced.

That dinosaur lasted for weeks! When it began to melt, it was the south side that melted first; the iced side held up much longer. Finally it melted enough for the head and neck to fall, but even then, the pile of snow was still called Buster. Eventually Buster was about teacup size and when next we looked, he was gone.

That's why our long-handled shovels are called "Buster," here on Whip-Poor-Will Hill.

Gene Waters took us for a ride in his motorcycle side car.

May Barton Meyers, my second mother, 1972.

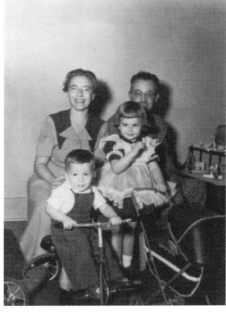

Santa brought a trycicle and a doll and buggy in 1952.

My beloved dad raised and sold fishing worms in retirement.

Time marches on! (1962)

After the drowning of our neighbor Walter Ray Brown, 9, I designed a safety post (left) for swimming spots that lacked supervision. It included easily accessible equipment strictly for rescue purposes. There is a life preserver in every vehicle—a spare tire floats (right). This was another of my water safety innovations.

I've ridden my Peugeot thousands of miles—3200 at age 58.

Sam's a wheel man at heart, whether on a bike or in a car.

Walt discovers a mishap after one of our salt firings.

Mary Starr Johnson-Gerard, Walt's wife

My stepgrandson Tim, dirty from firing the kiln.

Chris, Oliver, Peter, Cole, Jennifer, and Tim, six of my grandchildren, waiting for the school bus in 1991.

Chub collected and demonstrated old foot-powered tools, including this shaper.

In retirement I make old time pots to sell at Friends Together
Antiques. Photo by William Helvey

Examining the results of our eighteenth firing—fueled by wood, glazed with salt.

Breaking apart salt-glazed pots.

My brother Jim and his wife, Ella Mae—fun people who live near us.

While in Norway in 1971 my cycling students tricked me into this photo for my 57th birthday.

FOUR ROSES

It was Mother's Day and the kids came to my room snickering. "Happy Mother's Day, Mom," Nancy said as she handed me a lapel pin that was a pink and white metal rose. "Here," Walt said as he handed me a rose bush to plant. Then they read me a poem about four roses (a famous name of whiskey). The third rose was the card itself.

"Four roses," I said. "I just see three."

"Come outdoors and we'll show you," they said in unison. Off we went.

"Your fourth gift is Old Rose!" I'd been had! The kids had been trying to get me to OK their keeping an old hound dog which arrived on our farm uninvited, liked us, and decided to stay. I'd objected, but they named her Rose and begged, "Just until she has her puppies. You wouldn't want to send her away now?"

So, I received four roses for Mother's Day. Rose could stay "...till she has her babies and they're in good homes." Good old Rose presented us with seven little mixed breed hounds. As they grew to about six weeks, I had to keep reminding Nancy and Walt that she'd have to go and that we'd best be finding homes for the seven playful pups.

One pup was spotted like a Dalmatian and the kids named him Stripe. He went to one of our swimming pupils. We found a home for another one. Yet we still had five puppies and they were just about eating up poor old Rose!

While Chub and Walt were off on a trip to the World's Fair in New York, I called the Humane Society and asked if they'd take a female hound and five puppies—not a very attractive package actually. "Hold the phone," the fellow who answered said. "Yes, there's a fellow here now who'll take the mother and we'll have no trouble finding homes for the pups." So we loaded the family and sadly left them at the Humane Society.

On the way to church on Sunday morning, I found a flyer in the car that announced a big auction in Carrollton, Missouri, for that very day. Feeling footloose with the men away, I proposed that we go. Nancy was eager and so we stopped at church and got Barbara Smith, who was going to come home with us from church. We called her mom and off we went in our Sunday clothes.

We bought a lot of wonderful "junk" and as we were loading, I said to Barbara, "Go down to that old barn and look around for license plates. I'll bet you'll find a bunch stuck behind a post or something."

Off she went. Returning she said, mournfully, "No, there aren't any stuck up behind a post but THE WALL IS JUST PLASTERED WITH THEM!" I made a deal with the owner to pay 10 cents each for the plates. As we pulled nails and took down 52 plates, I spied the maple frame of a Lincoln rocker. Back to the porch I went to give the man $5.20 for the plates.

"Yes, I'd sell the old rocker. It ought to be worth another five dollar bill." Sold! We added it to our packed car and headed back to Columbia at almost dark.

It was really late when we finally pulled into our driveway. We came wide awake, however, when we were greeted by the wagging tail and soulful eyes of Old Rose!

We'll never know where that man took her, but Rose wanted to live with us and had found her way back "home." There was no way around it this time. Rose had found a permanent spot in our home and in our hearts.

"Four Roses"

Although we know
That you don't drink,
"Four Roses" we give
That wont put you in the klink.

One Rose is young
And stiff and Pink,
Another is old
And does she stink!

The last two Roses
Are in between,
They are pretty and red
and somell so keen!

So mother dear
As you will see,
With your "Four Roses"
How happy you'll be.

Happy Mom's Day   Nancy & W.E.

Aerial view of our farm in the 1980s.

A HIKE ON OUR FARM

SUNDAY, JUNE 15, 1958

Rain and community activities have kept us from being out and around the farm for a week, so our hike today was a real treat. Four inches of water accumulated in some of our neighbors' rain gauges and we certainly had that much here on our farm. (Uncle Archie's gauge has a hole in the bottom and it's disappointing to him to not know just exactly how much has fallen.) Terraces are standing full of water; grass and morning glories are growing in the corn field. The ponds are running over.

Chub and the kids started out this afternoon to check the growth of fescue and orchard grass and I tagged along in spite of tired legs from mowing the lawn. Walt complained of grass tickling his bare chest as we went through the timothy and fescue. The lespedeza wasn't a problem, however, as it is a low carpet only ankle deep. Our Pekingese, Fuey, bobbed along in the tall grass, just going and not knowing or caring where.

Beyond the barbed wire fence the cattle had eaten the pasture down low. Walt's chest was no longer being scratched, but his jeans kept sliding down showing how tanned his upper body was. His stride and swinging arms matched Chub's. Blackberries along the wooded waterway were green and swelling. I picked a typical sprig to show Unc. His hiking days are over but his interests are still keen, and we enjoy bringing things from the farm to show him.

Nancy and Walt lingered to enjoy the shelter and cool of the thicket. "Were these trees here in Jesus's time?" Nancy asked. We decided that the damp, spongy earth underfoot was rich with the decayed trees and leaves that may well have grown two thousand years ago.

Hurrying to catch up with Chub, we found him looking at the sod that heals earth scars of the past. When we bought our farm, Chub and Dad plowed in and leveled some ditches that were deeper than the height of the tractor and they stopped further erosion with terraces and waterways. Strips of red clay on which almost no grass will grow reminded us of the barren field of five years ago. When we bought the farm, my Dad advised, "Just say you're buying 80 acres. The east half is worth what you'll pay for the entire 160 acres, but this west 80 will have to rush to make enough to pay its taxes." Today the field is gently rolling. Two ponds remind us of the deepest gullies, but today's orchard grass, timothy and lespedeza are lush enough to be cut and baled soon.

Short, shaggy Fuey drank from cow tracks and terraces. The sun occasionally peeped out between clouds that were hurrying northeastward. It's been several days since it has warmed our backs and I envied Fuey as he lapped the cool water. He got tangled in some dewberry briars that hug the ground along the creek diversion terrace but Nancy carried him through. She loves that dog and didn't seem to mind scratching her legs to rescue him from the stickers.

The cattle looked good. They were knee deep in pasture and the pond was running over. Chub had put a chunk of sod in a small groove that had grown enough to cut out and empty the pond. With weary legs, we climbed the driveway hill back to the house. The sky was a deep blue with cotton pillow clouds drifting over the horizon. Birds chattered in the mulberry tree and an occasional ripe berry dropped onto the purple stained lawn below. The house looked especially white, the lawn a greener green and the roses a deeper red because of the recent, wonderful rain. "This is it," I thought as the children raced ahead to raid the icebox before supper. Chub and I followed in the raid and I served Unc a plate in front of the TV.

The perfect event of this perfect Sunday was still to come. An hour before sunset I got my fly rod, stopped in the barn lot to dig a dozen fat worms, and slipped out to the pond behind the house. I did not slip quietly enough to be alone, however, for just as I dropped my line in the water, I saw Walt coming over the pond bank. A big bluegill snapped my line and I yelled, "Get the stringer quick. I've latched onto a granddaddy!" I baited his line as he ran for the stringer and he caught a bass before I had landed the bluegill. By dark we'd had a couple of big ones get away, had caught several little ones for the cats and had saved enough fish to clean for tomorrow night's supper.

Surely Heaven can't be better than this!

Uncle Archie came for a week and stayed four years.

UNC QUOTES MCGUFFEY

After wiring up some broken fence, sweat stood out on Uncle Archie's forehead and on the top of his bald head. We learned a lot from Unc. What a fun man!

"Did you have the story of Meddlesome Mattie in McGuffey's First Reader?" he asked, as he rested and rocked and smoked his morning cigar. I told him that I didn't even have McGuffey's Reader. Unc often said it was hard to beat old McGuffey.

Seems Meddlesome Mattie got into her grandmother's snuff and "She had it in her eyes and nose and chin and as the snuff got farther in, Mattie sure repented."

Unc also quoted the Bible a lot to support some point he wanted to make. He often defined a good woman. "She riseth before the dawn and goeth about preparing food and drink for her husband." I told him many times, "I'm not that woman!"

For Walt, a second grader, he quoted from his old arithmetic book: "Walt, if a man pays 10 cents a pint for liquor and drinks a pint a day for 27 years and dies of his folly, what is the cost of the liquor?"

"His life!" the boy replied promptly.

DOWN-TO-EARTH FUN

"Mother! Mother! Guess what we're doing? We're having more fun!"

"Oh?" I answered halfheartedly, "What?"

"Walt and I are telling stories to the fishing worms."

Right then and there I stopped my work and took the children fishing.

Two things ran through my mind that day and made me stop and enjoy my kids. First, they were always collecting fishing worms in a jar or a can, but that usually was the end of it. "Mother is too busy right now..." Second, this is the kind of fun that country kids have—spontaneous, imaginative, homemade fun with little equipment or organization—down-to-earth fun. How much "downer" can you get than telling stories to earth-worms?

MABLE MIRED IN THE MUD

In the short time between arriving home from work and before total darkness, Chub changed to coveralls and said, "Kids, let's drive over to see if the wheat has come up." I welcomed a few minutes alone before fixing supper. But Chub was soon back with that look that farm wives dread.

"You'll have to help. Old Bones is mired down in the pond."

Old Bones is registered as "Mabel the Fourth" and she's Nancy's beloved 4-H cow. She got the nickname as a tease from Walt, but Bones is healthy, fat and strong. At least she was before this catastrophe.

Chub went to the barn for a cable, some ropes and gunny sacks; we then headed for the disaster area by tractor. Nancy was in tears when we arrived and Walt was trying to devise a way to get her out. The back third of that cow was in the silt and water. She had pawed and flopped around for at least a day and a night. She looked at us with staring, frightened eyes and seemed too weak to make the effort to move.

Chub looped the rope around her neck and padded it with sacks. Then he tied the rope to the cable and attached the cable to the tractor. I was to drive and had lined up the tractor in the direction of the desired pull. We all knew, but no one said it, that one mishap would end it for the beloved animal, which was Nancy's pride and joy.

Chub waded deep into the water and mud and grabbed Bones by the tail; he nodded for me to pull as he gave a mighty heave on her tail. But when her neck stretched enough to pull her head forward with eyes bugging out, I chickened out and let the cable go slack. After a moment I was composed and Chub gave the signal again. I moved that tractor forward ever so gently. Old Bones floundered at the right time and Chub's extra boost on her rear all worked together and out she came! I continued to drag until she was well away from the water and on to dry grass.

Chub came sloshing out of the mud and silt and Nancy threw her arms around Bones' muddy neck and thanked her for helping at the right time. The cow was too weak to get up on her feet. We feared she might be paralyzed from being in the pond so long. Chub and I comforted Nancy and he said, "We'll have the Vet come out in the morning, but for now we must get her some grain and a bale of hay."

"And a tarp to keep her warm," Nancy added.

We all four rode the tractor back to the house. I scrubbed, changed clothes and went to fix supper while the kids and Chub took the oil lantern, food and bedding back to the pasture to make Bones more comfortable for the night. I kept the food warm while they cleaned up. Supper was late of course. No homework was done. The piano practice wasn't even mentioned and we all bathed and went to bed exhausted.

The next morning Old Bones was standing almost steady on

her feet, munching her food. Things are really looking brighter on Whip-Poor-Will Hill this day. And, yes, the little green needles of wheat are sticking up out of the ground and dew drops on them reflected the light as the warm sun rose to dry them and help them grow.

The fiddle is not exactly like a violin, and I was never a violinist.

LADY FIDDLER

Miss Frances Grindstead met me in the hall and said, "Why don't you come to my office soon and we'll work on your 'Fiddles' piece and submit it in the Atlantic Monthly's essay contest for College Students." She was my instructor in special writing at the University of Missouri's School of Journalism—a very good one, as the next paragraph will prove.

She made the same offer to at least two other students and all three of us were winners. Charles won the first prize, I won the second and Daphne was third in the national contest! That was in 1936, the year I graduated. Here is the essay Miss Grindstead submitted in the contest:

FIDDLES
By Sue Emelyn Meyers, University of Missouri

How it happened I don't know, but there I was, crowded into one corner of a nine-by-twelve room with dozens of other people crowded into that same nine-by-twelve, and all but the eight dancers were looking at me. Even they cast admiring glances in my direction whenever they could spare a minute from their stomping and whirling.

It was the first time they had heard a girl play honest-to-goodness fiddling tunes on an honest-to-goodness fiddle. Oh yes, there was Dewey's oldest girl who went off to school; she learned to play "Turkey in the Straw," but she learned it out of a book. And it sounded like book-music, too.

"Wal, by gollys," the guitar picker mused between tobacco spats, "it sounds just like them guys ye hear on the raddio." That was a real compliment to my fiddling. All I could do was smile to myself and try to manufacture some excuse for being there other than that I was an egoist who was more content to be the idol of a crowd of toothless square dancers than just one of the bunch of college seniors back on the campus.

But fiddler I am. I'm proud of it, too, though I sometimes feel a little ashamed that those few ergs of talent weren't directed to some other line of musical development that would have been of more use to society. Why, I could be teaching grade schoolers to sing the "Star Spangled Banner"; but I'm not. Instead, I'm sawing off "Chicken Reel" over and over again on a valuable instrument that might be playing "Salute d'Amour" or a Kreisler composition. My instrument ranks with my playing: among the finest in the fiddle world, but rather subordinate in the world of violins and violinists.

When I was in the sixth grade, my parents put forth every effort to make a violinist of me, but an uncle who loved the old hoedowns persuaded me to quit practicing scales and learn a real piece, like "Ragtime Annie."

What a surprise it was to Mother when she returned from the club one day and found wire strings on my lovely violin, which had begun a metamorphosis into a regular fiddle. What a surprise, too, when she found a few weeks later, that I had tightened my bow into a slightly convex curve and had not unwound it after playing. I was buying regular fiddler's rosin in the bulk at a hardware store and had given my violinists rosin (wrapped in chamois skin and packed in an aluminum box) to a chum who was still practicing those silly scales.

I laid aside my leather music case (with my name on in gold) and folded my handwritten fiddling tunes to fit my violin case, which was rapidly coming to be known as a fiddle box.

Nothing Mother could say would convince me that I should give up this "fool idea" and return to the scales. My twelve-year-old determination was further augmented the first time Uncle Charlie heard the "Little Brown Jug" from my own nimble fingers.

I soon learned that there was an art to this fiddling and that it wasn't all just "a lot of scratching around," as violinists see it; there was never a doubt about my art among those people packed into the corners of this room in which the floor heaved up and down as the caller patted out the set. Four sweating farmers and four perspiring farmers' wives were having the time of their lives. Onlookers from outside the house were snuffing out any breeze that had a chance to sneak by their heads, through the window. I was going over great!

What if some of the kids at MU could see me now! Yes I thought with a sickening glub in my throat, what if they should! With that I missed a note and would have lost the beat except for the stamping of dancers' feet. The guitar picker had long since lost all consciousness of the smoke-filled room full of overalled onlookers. Lucky fellow, too, for a fiddler can't go off like that. He can't even chew gum and keep on fiddling. One mix-up on the bowing of a piece and the entire rhythm and melody are lost.

That's why you can't learn to play square dances from a book. Every fiddler has his own particular way of bowing a piece, and though it seems to an observer that he is most concerned with the fingering of the left hand, it is actually the bowing that makes the difference between good fiddling and bad. I was once interrupted in the middle of a square dance, and, though my bowing only stopped for a second, I could not pick up the tune and had to begin the piece again. A fiddler does not play with reckless abandon, but with a skill that no violinist can ever attain.

From the very beginning, a violinist is taught to place his fingers firmly on the strings in the exact tone position. But even the beginning fiddler knows that the way to produce a good rolling tone is by sliding from a lower halftone into the position of the ultimate note. The fiddler, consequently, cannot leave his fingers on the note until he needs that note again as the violinist does, for he has to raise them to get ready for another slide into position.

So inborn is the art of fiddling that it cannot be taught. I learned by following an Ozarkian fiddler as he played for dances in my home community. I sat by him for hours until I finally got the hang of fiddling and then went home to work it out for myself.

A fiddler can't wait till it's convenient for him to practice a new tune. When it first starts running through his head, he has to sit right down and work out the coordination between fingers and bow. That's the way it is in learning to play. You have to take one piece and play it over and over until you're good at it before you stop. One fiddler I know will stop his car in the road and get his fiddle out to try over a new tune that has just come to him.

Every chance I got, I would grab a fiddle at intermissions of our dances and pick up a few vital pointers from the guitar pickers. I was surprised when I found out that a fiddler does not stop playing a square dance when he gets tired, but must go on until he breaks a string or until the dance ends (which is practically never).

The climax of my fiddling career came one night when I was in a strange community (Moscow Mills, Mo.) and was scratching around during intermission. When the real fiddler came back and heard me he said, "Say, why don't you play one and let me and my gal dance?" Before I knew what I was doing, I had agreed. I knew that I could not last till the finish, but I had been hoping for this chance since the first time I played "Little Brown Jug."

Six sets were arranged in the hayloft dance hall. The dance began and I played "Golden Slippers" over and over until I thought I should turn into one. No one even dreamed that I was likely to collapse any minute. A cramp crept up my back like a serpent and my bow hand was so numb that I wondered if I wasn't paralyzed. Just at the crucial moment, two Bohemians became entangled over a partner and the dancers stopped to watch the fun. After a five-minute intermission in which the pieces of the Bohemians were lugged outside, the dancing was resumed and I finished the set apparently without struggle. They think I'm a great little fiddler down there; they'll never know that I had never played for a complete square before.

Before I quit playing that night, I noticed a burly, unshaven man watching my every move; I was becoming uneasy under his stare when he ventured to the "orchestra pit" and said, "Sister, you'll never have to work for a living." I knew that I was made!

As if fiddling weren't work! After four hours, that ever-recurrent pain strikes my girlish backbone just as it did that night in the hayloft, and settles there for the rest of the evening.

Four hours of fiddling is only a start at a real square dance. The farmers collect as soon as the cows are milked and the chickens fed and locked up for the night; they seem never to stop dancing. Not a single Ford is wound up and headed for home until the host has treated with coffee, cake, and sandwiches of country-cured ham on home made bread. The men drink so much home brew on the back porch that it's up to the women to get the kids bundled up and persuade their husbands to go home, which is hardly ever before 2:30 a.m.

I often wonder what it would have been like if I had kept practicing scales. What would these farmers think of mellow tones produced by a well-haired bow on silver and gut strings instead of the sharp rasping ones produced by a greasy bow on steel? How could I manage to keep my instrument tuned with the ebony pegs that are now replaced with patented metal nonslip ones? How out-of-place those hobnail boots would be on a hardwood dance floor after being accustomed to this splintered nine-by-twelve bedroom! Would "Marmaduke's Horn pipe" carry above the noise of the dancers if my fiddle were tuned down two tones to universal pitch, which violinists use? No, the other fiddlers would think I had gone sissy on them, just as they would if I trimmed my bridge as violinists do, to where it would be just as easy to reach the farthest strings as the nearer ones.

Not a one would dance, even though I played the same tunes, in the same rhythm, if I held the instrument as violinists do, on my shoulder and collar bone rather than on my upper arm, and if I grasped the bow by the frog rather than midway between the frog and the tip. Suppose my accompanist sat at a Steinway instead of a $3.98 mail-order-house guitar? In my dreams I raise my bow to caress the silver strings of my valuable violin, but the master of ceremonies interrupts me as he hands me a sweat stained hat with $3.87 in small change in it— my pay for the night's performance!

12 MILES FROM TOWN

OLD WOMAN, OLD DOG AND DEER AT DAWN

Cicero wrote about the green of the meadows, the trees, the beauty of vineyards and the olive groves. "For where can old age find more genial warmth of sunshine or fire ... more cooling shade or more refreshing waters?"

Thank you, Miss Eva Johnston, for introducing me to that old philosopher in your Latin class. His message prepared me for a morning like this.

Misty and I walked down our one-lane country road before sunup, just as four deer walked out of the woods in single file. I stood motionless, admiring them, but the old dog did not see, smell or hear those beautiful does. They too, stood motionless staring at Misty and me. I scratched the dog's neck to keep her quiet and marveled at their immaculate satin coats, their broad ears sticking out wide to catch every sound, those spindly legs and tiny hooves. Four bronze statues, tails at rest! Finally they walked slowly across the road, munched a few bites and then, one at a time, sprung up and over the barbed wire fence, to the woods side. Their short tails stuck straight up in the air for a moment, the white underneath flashing as they floated for a moment en route.

At first I could see only two, then three, finally all four deer blended in with the natural tans of dry leaves, trees and brush in the woods. They hid themselves in a frozen pose, looking back. I was posed too, except for my fingers caressing the dog's neck. Finally I started walking slowly and quietly, hoping they'd not stir.

Stop! A huge buck streaked across our path, muscles rippling, antlers balanced and front legs reaching far forward. Without hesitating he floated over the barbed wire and into the brush. All five deer disappeared as if they'd melted away. What a sight!

I've seen few buck deer close up like that. One raced our car one time when we surprised him around a sharp bend in the lane. He had been grazing in our hayfield and turned too fast to turn into the woods. For almost a quarter of a mile it was nip and tuck but we slowed to let him make a getaway.

I'd never been as close to a beautiful buck as I was to this one. He had waited in the woods until his females were safely across the road, over the fence and into the heavy cover of the woods. He started across just as Misty and I moved to resume our walk. It must take courage to protect four females in the wild!

Old Cicero recognized that the lives of old people are enriched by the freedom to stroll among the trees and vineyards at dawn.

Turning from the county road into our private lane I silently said: "Thank you, Miss Johnston and Cicero, for leading me to this place, late in life, and this time, with deer in my green meadow and grove of trees."

HARD FREEZE TONIGHT

When the weatherman predicts "There'll be a hard freeze tonight," we usually shift our priorities and rush to pick the remaining garden vegetables. Boone County's first hard freeze usually comes in mid to late October.

Peppers, tomatoes, okra, melons, and other vegetables are enjoying a sudden growing spurt just now. The pepper plants are bending under the weight of new growth. Cantaloupe vines are blooming, and okra and tomatoes are outdoing themselves, as if they sense the end is near.

Lots of the ripe tomatoes and green peppers go to the kitchen; almost-ripe and green tomatoes go to our in-the-ground cellar. We sometimes pull the cherry tomato plants up by the roots and pile them on a shelf in the cellar. With luck there'll be a few left for a salad on Thanksgiving day.

One Friday morning, almost forty years ago, the early morning forecast was "There'll be a hard freeze tonight." Uncle Archie said he'd help me take care of the vegetables before Chub and the kids came home. He's a lot of help around the farm and we're glad he came to live with us.

I got some baskets and buckets ready for the picking and then remembered that Chub asked me to take a bit of corn to the hogs. Just then Unc came in with a bucket of Skyline's warm milk to strain.

As he sat the bucket on the cabinet, he said casually, "Save out some for the white sow; she had seven baby pigs this morning." Then he added, "We'd better mix the milk with some 'ship stuff.' She left the shed and had those pigs right out on the cold damp ground, up against the wire fence."

He said, "I'll get straw while you mix the feed." As I mixed the ship stuff I accepted the fact that shivering piglets have priority over tomatoes and peppers.

We didn't dare try to move the sow and piglets. When a sow wants to have her babies out in the cold, it's best to leave her alone for a while; some sows will kill their own offspring when upset.

Unc, a heavyset man with wobbly legs, and I put together baling wire and pliers to tie a large piece of galvanized roofing to the fence for a windbreak. The sow scolded us for this and for putting straw around her and her seven pink piggies.

Next I started the tractor to go to the corn field, but a front tire was low, so I drove to the shed to use the compressor. Once the tire was filled we were on our way to shuck enough corn for our pet sow, Woodchuck, who was due to have her first litter next week, and a few hogs that would soon go to market.

Returning with the sack of corn, we found that Woodchuck was crowding in with the white sow and her new babies. She wouldn't be driven away, so Unc enticed her to follow a scoop of ear corn and we eased her through the gate and latched it quickly behind her. Maybe her babies would arrive tonight! We got Skyline out of the lot because a pig can get mashed by a milk cow's hoof.

Unc and I stopped for a late cup of soup and a cold beef sandwich. When we checked the residents of the barn lot next, things were quiet and unchanged—except for the screeching of new baby kittens! We searched the barn and found "Betty" behind some machinery, licking two new kittens. The kids would soon be walking up our long driveway from the school bus so I quickly warmed a wool rag and wrapped the chilled kittens. Betty and babies were sound asleep in a shoe box on the open oven door when Nancy and Walt gladly took over as nurse maids.

Near midnight I ended my journal entry by saying: "It's been a busy day. The wind quit blowing as a cool front passed at noon and the air seems fresher and purer than ever. It was one of those beautiful crisp October days with trees turning and birds singing. We've saved seven baby pigs and four unwanted kittens."

And yes, we got most (but not all) of the tomatoes and peppers picked before night and the hard freeze that's predicted.

CHUB'S SOLUTION

"What shall I fix for our weekend guests?" I asked Chub. "What kind of meals would you suggest?"

"What do you mean?" he asked.

"Well, what meat, for starters?" I asked.

His puzzled look told me that he'd never thought about the planning that goes in to having company. He finally dismissed the topic by saying, "Oh, I don't know. Why do you worry about things like that? That'll take care of itself. (Pause) It always does!"

THE CABIN ON OUR FARM

1966

It's a short thirty minutes from our house to town and the new road section that is being built will shorten that time even more. I can't help thinking of the distance it was by spring wagon, when the Robnetts petitioned this farm from the government. For all I know, that was before the spring wagon day—but it was a long way from town, without a doubt.

There's an old family burial ground across the road from our place and the kids and I sometimes read the markers and wonder about life here, over 100 years ago. Some of the people buried there were born almost 200 years ago. Most are relatives by blood or marriage, except for the prewar slaves. The land abstract records the gift of a slave girl to one landowner's crippled daughter.

Reading the monuments, we're struck by the number of youngsters who didn't make it to maturity. It would have been a long way to town to get a doctor in case of an inflamed appendix or summer complaint or diphtheria. Those mothers got along without paper hankies, bottle warmers, plastic pants and bathinettes; but it's hard to imagine getting along without protective "shots."

When we bought this farm there was an old log house that was falling in. It had sheltered people for over 150 years. A road was changed and the cabin was reversed; the back became the front. This left the cistern pump on the front porch and the windows all on the backside. We had engaged a bulldozer to clean out some hedge trees and old fencerows. We decided it would also be a good time to have the old house pushed in. It could then be burned and we could clean the spot in our side yard. Chub drug off some of the better logs and used them for a base for a haystack. What was left of the old log house looked like an easy pushover for a bulldozer that had just uprooted ancient and reluctant hedge trees.

But we hadn't reckoned with the ingenuity and engineering skills of the pioneers who trimmed those interlocking notches in the huge timbers. That house was put up to stay up and it stayed up in spite of all that bulldozer could do. The Diesel engine roared, the bulldozer bore down on the weakest corner, loose timbers shook and what was left of the roof fell in. That old log house, however, still stood straight and proud, not defeated by a modern machine. I can't help comparing its strength to the strength of those folks buried in the family cemetery on the hill.

SPRING'S A GAME OF "WHO'S FIRST?"

This is the time of the year when we compete with Mother Nature and with our neighbors to see who can be first. For example, we had our first asparagus last week, our cabbage and broccoli plants (frozen and flooded as they are) put on their first real growth, and we were first in how much the rain gauge registered after the big rain.

My neighbor was first in how big their hailstones were and we were lucky because we didn't get a one! The last big hail was years ago and I decided to gather up some of the largest. That isn't easy because I got battered with the ones that fell while I was still sorting out smaller ones for larger treasures. I put about a dozen in the freezer and had proof, all summer, that our hailstones were really big—not like golf balls at all because each one was several stones frozen into single, irregular clump.

Mr. William McHarg used to take a first pink radish to church and show it off while the congregation was singing. I couldn't do that when my claim to fame was enormous heads of broccoli and cauliflower. April and May produce a lot of firsts; however what we miss most is the old time delicious tastes.

How many people under thirty have gone to their very own strawberry patch and eaten one fresh picked, right off the vine? Many have, of course, but it isn't the thrill it used to be because we have strawberries all year long! Shipped in ones, frozen ones, and chunks of strawberry in our ice cream cones can't match the taste of that very first shiny one eaten warm and unwashed from your own strawberry patch.

It's the same with spinach, radishes, grapes and zucchini. By late summer we'll be hard put to find anyone who'd like another zucchini, but I'll enjoy the first of that because I'm too frugal to pay the price for a little banana-sized zucchini in the stores, off season. I was pretty dumb not to plant a lot of quick-growing lettuce in a big flower pot this year. Last year I did that and picked lettuce leaves as fast as they matured. I chose head lettuce this time, and it has survived the cold and wet but it's just begun to grow.

As the summer progresses, we'll look forward to our first sweet corn. This is one that air freight and freezers can't match. Our neighbor treats us to sweet corn that's planted four long rows at a time, once a week for as long as it has a chance to mature. Raccoons know when it's at its best and their heavy weight breaks stalks down to where they can eat the corn on the ground. We watch for coon damage and pick our first ears as soon as we see their trash between rows.

So important is the competition for the first tomato that I'm willing to buy three or four of those started plants—already blooming—potted and ready to be transplanted. The problem with this is, my competitors do the same. I learned it from them! ✍

WHAT'S "SHIP STUFF"?

MAY 5, 1958

We overslept by about 10 minutes this morning and as Chub hurried off to work he called back to me, "Oh, you'll have time to slop the red sow, won't you?" Of course I would or her babies would get hungry! "Stir up that ship stuff that's in the can and give her a bucketful." Simple as that—five minutes would probably do the trick.

I slipped out of my shoes and into Chub's cold rubber boots, which bumped my knees fore and aft as I walked. The calendar says May and the poets are writing of birds, flowers and warm breezes, but they're not on Whip-Poor-Will Hill this morning. Two inches of rain have fallen in the last two days and a March-like wind is whipping the drizzle across the barn lot at blizzard velocities. The cats, half frozen, squat in balls around the back door. Our lone rooster crows to keep warm.

I find the baby pigs asleep in a stack, so wrapped around each other that I can't count the same number twice. At intervals they shiver, all nine or ten of them at the same time. Their mother grunts as she roots through corn cobs hoping for a few overlooked grains from yesterday.

"Stir the ship stuff in the can..." What can? I locate a large garbage can. The sacks in the shed hold ground corn chop, ammonium nitrate fertilizer, bone meal and dark red animal mineral.

So, being of a creative nature and loving to stir up a mess, I begin to concoct something edible for a mother of nine or ten baby pigs. I put in handfuls of chop, a glob of bone meal, and half a handful of the expensive mineral; amounts determined by cost, no doubt. Last of all I stir in enough water to make a thick gruel. The sound of my stirring attracts the sow. She slurps so eagerly as I pour the slop into the trough that some of it goes right on her head. Just for good measure and to make up for the messy head, I throw in six ears of corn to tide her over. Her happy grunts serve as a thank you for my questionable concoction.

I stop with my back to the wind and observe this May day. The clouds are rolling and breaking away and I hear the creek roaring. I know it's a muddy red. In contrast, the grass is a bright green. Ponds that were not visible from this spot last summer are now bank full. The beating rain has softened some of the scars of winter: ruts where the cornpicker and tractor crossed the front yard, where cattle tracked through the lawn in search of Spring's early grass and where the pickup got stuck when snow hid the driveway. I glance at my garden and see the radishes have their third leaves but are looking kind of battered because of the near hail of yesterday's cloudburst.

I step through the obstacle course of cold cats and stomp the muddy manure off Chub's boots. I enjoy the warm feeling of a job well done as I start my familiar chores of the day, even if I still don't know the recipe for that "ship stuff!"

A MESSAGE IN THE SNOW

One winter day in the 1970s, Floyd Kaiser and Willis Smith came over to cut wood with Chub. We were eating lunch when I asked, "Has anybody seen Misty? She didn't go to the woods with you men, did she?"

"No," they said. "She barked at me when I drove in," one man said.

I left the table to call and whistle for her, but she didn't come running around the house as usual. Later I called the neighbors, but no one had seen her. By late afternoon she had not returned and I drove the country roads looking for her. Near dark, Chub and I drove over the snowy white pastures, near enough to see that Misty, a large black dog, wasn't in one of Denny's traps.

We asked Denny, our close friend and a responsible trapper, to trap here because coyotes become a threat to livestock during the coldest part of the winter when their natural food is scarce. After dark I remembered that he had placed an additional trap a few days before. I called him and said, "Old Misty has been missing since mid-morning and we've checked your other traps, but where is the new one set?" He said it was over in the northeast corner of the farm, and we hadn't been near that.

I opened the gate while Chub brought the truck and away we went. When we got to the top of the hill behind the pond, we saw two eyes reflecting and bounding up and down. Old Misty was alive and she knew we had found her. How could she jump around like that and still be held in that heavy coyote trap?

I grabbed the big dog and held tight. "Hold still, Misty, we're going to get you out," but she kept jumping.

Chub was trying to get the heavy steel trap in position to step on it and release the dog. Misty wasn't about to calm down. The trap flopped around as she licked me and kept jumping. Chub kept turning and twisting to get the trap in position to release her and suddenly he said, "Oh! I've got a leg cramp!" I couldn't have sprung that trap even with no dog in it. By the time Misty calmed down a bit, Chub had a cramp in both legs!

I don't know how we got out of that mess, but we did. Coyotes, small prairie wolves, are wild members of the dog family. Misty had smelled the strong scent spread near the trap. She must have pawed at the trap because it caught her just beyond the toes. She limped a little for the next two or three days, but was otherwise fine.

Denny always runs his traps about daybreak. He stopped one morning when there was new snow on the ground and said, "You just must drive down to that bottomland and see where the coyotes have been playing 'fox and geese.'"

Chub and I drove down and, sure enough, they had tramped out a huge circle and crossed it with several "spokes" like we do for the tag game we play in snow. The fox tries to tag the geese and, if tagged, the goose becomes the fox. No one can get off the wheel pattern and the geese are safe when they're in the "nest" where spokes cross.

The coyotes had spokes crossing the circle, but there was no sign of a nest. There were not many other tracks disturbing the white blanket of snow, except where the coyotes had played the game.

We learned this game from Indians. Perhaps they learned it from coyotes playing in snow in our very own pasture?

A snowy Whip-Poor-Will Hill with Snip, Archie and sleigh.

Wartime fly fishing in Michigan.

A HANDFUL OF WORMS

SPRING 1985

You'd think that at age 70+ years I'd have finally learned that it is almost impossible to hoe or rake while holding a bunch of wiggly grubs in my hand. But no, I found myself picking up the ones which squirmed out of my grip. I finally walked across the garden to the big container where I've stockpiled fishing worms for glorious days on the pond bank with my grandsons.

Picking up worms isn't always successful, but I have to do it. It is a part of me—like sowing oats was a part of old-time farmers. In spring they just had to sow oats, even if the market was terrible and they didn't have a team of horses to feed through the winter. Something stirs in the farmer and creates a real anticipation of things to come, whatever that might be.

So it is with grubs and worms. The urge to chuck the work and hurry over to the pond bank is postponed if I have a container in which to collect worms. My work becomes a quest instead of work. Actually, if it weren't too windy today to cast a line or to maneuver the canoe, I wouldn't be resisting. After all, at this age, who cares?

Peter, Cole, and Oliver (from left) creating fun with an old rag mop head while crushing clay for Granny.

WHATEVER HAPPENED TO OLD FASHIONED FUN?

A mother of eight once told me that she never paid much attention to the kids' arguments until she saw blood; but against her advice, I went to see why my two preschool grandsons were raising their voices at each other. They were tugging at an empty plastic bottle I'd put on "their" shelf in the back room. They also were playing with those empty black film canisters and cardboard paper towel tubes. The floor was ankle deep in Darth Vaders and Jedi stuff as well as those sexy, muscular men who are trying (or did they already succeed?) in mastering the Universe.

After teaching principles of creative recreation for 25 years, I bite my tongue as my grandsons wind things up, push switches and follow a toy across the room as it does something—climbing, crawling or flip flopping. My nature tells me that the boys, not their toys, should be climbing, crawling and flip flopping!

When the Sears Christmas Wishbook came (around Halloween!), I spent some time studying it to see what boys do these days. What do boys do? They stretch out on their tummies and watch! Page after page showed these catalog kids having "fun," sitting cross-legged with hands on hips or chins, "playing" at watching some mechanical thing do something. Where were the jumping ropes, the roller skates? Climbing ropes? Scooters? I bought a scooter at a junk shop because I couldn't find one at the toy store. The boys were fascinated. "What is it?" "How do you do it?" "Where's the other wheel?"

"It's an antique," I explained, as I got one foot on and pushed off down the sidewalk. My trip was stopped short by two boys who couldn't wait to try it.

There's no happy ending to all of this. Nobody advertises scooters on Saturday morning TV. The paper towel tubes and plastic bottles will soon be at the bottom of the toy box under the purple muscle men and Star Wars stuff. Come to think of it, they may even be out of style by now. I didn't watch the Saturday morning shows this week.

HELICOPTER IN THE FRONT YARD

In 1988 Paul Shankman, of Channel 2 in St. Louis, called to ask if he could film an interview for his weekly program called "Neighbors." I was pleased that he wanted to write about my digging local white clay and sculpting "little people." We agreed that he would come at 1 p.m. on February 21. When he asked directions to our farm, he said, "We'll be coming by helicopter, of course."

I'd never thought about directions from the air, but he said they'd be flying low enough to see the highway exit signs so I described our buildings, pools and the small lake behind the house. "If you have any trouble locating us," I said, "just go to the Regional Airport and I'll come to meet you."

This promised to be an exciting event so our Nancy and Walt brought their boys who were 5, 6 and two who were 9 years old. We bundled up and went out to watch for the helicopter to arrive. Standing on the pond bank, we saw one finally come in view, but it went east of our place and kept going in spite of our yelling and waving. I wondered how they could have missed our "white house with green roof near two swimming pools and a small lake." But they did miss us.

Paul Shankman called from the airport and Nancy and I drove the three miles to meet him while I worried that the boys might not see the helicopter after all. Paul rode with us, though, and the chopper flew overhead, zigzagging back and forth to keep from outrunning us. In sight of our place, the pilot made a beeline for the spot I'd described as being free of power lines and a good place to land—about 20 yards in front of our picture window. The helicopter was gently setting down, creating a blizzard with the propellers blowing the unexpected snow from the night before. Walt and the boys were lined up on the sidewalk out of the way. The boys, in motionless disbelief, had mouths open, hands and arms hanging limp and bodies stretched forward toward the helicopter. Oh, for a photo of that!

After an hour's chat, the photographer said, "The light's just right for the filming of digging the clay." They wanted to use the outdoor shots at the opening and closing of the film segment.

The pilot visited with Chub and the boys while I drove the men to the clay site. The photographer shot some footage as Paul asked questions along the way. Meanwhile, the boys asked the pilot if they could "touch the helicopter." That wasn't enough for Oliver, age five, who said, "I want to ride in it!" The pilot (who had flown in Vietnam and Korea) explained that a ride wasn't permitted but that they could get inside. When we returned, Oliver said, "Granny, I DROVE the helicopter."

When Paul had the story, they stayed and visited until almost dark. Because our satellite did not include Channel 2 in St. Louis, Chub and I drove to High Hill and viewed the program with our friend Vera, who worked at the plant where we buy bulk clay that I use for making pottery.

Paul Shankman covered it all in less than three minutes! He was fascinated that I was an old woman, that Dr. Henry Heimlich came here to see my sculptures of historical artificial respiration and that I taught swimming. He even used a bathing suit snapshot from the 1930s.

As we reviewed the event, Oliver said, "I thought he'd see me waving because I had on my red gloves." And Walt determined why they couldn't find our farm from the air: the previous night's snow had turned everything white!

A cloudy day at Whip-Poor-Will Hill in 1998.

COWS COME HOME

This is the day our farm breathes back to life. No Kansas snow is blowing through here on its way to Illinois. There are no skaters under star-studded black skies at night. No ice-covered cedar trees are bent to the ground.

Instead, May apples curtsy to morels, asparagus raises its head. Coyotes screech and our two dogs reply promptly. Redbud and wild pear nod in March's ballet, sweet anemones dance with violets and dutchman's britches. And the cows come home!

They're back from muddy feed lots, back to rolling pastures. But trouble comes along. Mothers run down slippery truck ramps. Bawling, calling, running into fences, shouting, "Bay-bee! ... Bay-bee?" Searching, fearing, they keep calling "Bay-bee?"

Suddenly 50 anxious mothers – quiet, listening, motionless, silent.
Mamas face the fence looking, hearing! Half a mile away, how

do they possibly know?   Truck's a'coming ... with BABIES!
Still not in sight, but these mothers DO know!

Finally anxious, frightened babies stumble off the down ramp
crying, "Ma-a-ma?' Ma-a-a-a-ma!"   Mamas come a'running.
Butting, big bags bobbing side-to-side.
All are smelling, finally finding, that special one.   Babies slurping.   Slobbers drooling.

Mamas licking, loving, resting.   Babies bellies bulging.
Cows and calves are quiet, seeking quiet places.
Suddenly this farm is resuscitated.

And I am too! 🐄

"LEAVES THREE, TURN AND FLEE" —OR ELSE!

A friend and I were returning from a late summer weekend in the Ozarks and we stopped to let our grade school children eat, run and wade in a creek. Julie saw some bright red leaves – the first touch of autumn color. "Sue, come see this beautiful vine," she called as she fingered the shiny, waxy leaves.

"Julie, come away! That's poison ivy," I screamed.

"Oh, no," she argued, "I know poison ivy." I recited the old warning, "Leaves three, turn and flee, leaves five, let it thrive," as I coaxed her away from that climbing vine. Several days later she called to say, "That was poison ivy!"

This plant defends itself from being picked, crushed, cut, dug up, stepped on or even just lightly touched. Animals can carry the offending oil, but they don't get the rash or blisters. People are affected in varying degrees – but I shudder to hear someone say, "Oh, I don't get it." That could change.

Luckily, I've had only two really bad encounters. Old timers said I should eat three or four ivy leaves early each spring to develop immunity. "Horrors! What about my poor stomach?" I'd say. Others advised, "There's nothing to prevent it, you just have to stay out of the woods."

Me? Stay out? The woods was my childhood playground and the source of my spending money. I picked violets and gooseberries in spring; blackberries in mid-July; hazelnuts, hickory nuts and black walnuts in the fall; leaf mold for flower beds any time of the year. Mom and I loved the woods and went there often. She often reviewed the "leaves three" rhyme and showed me the stuff from a distance. I learned to avoid three-leaf ivy and its relative, poison oak, which was more of a bush but still had three leaves and the poisonous oil.

I must have let my guard down at age 14 while picking blackberries. Ivy rash, itchy and with blisters, covered my hands, arms, ankles and part of my face. Not only did it itch uncontrollably, it oozed and dripped for several days. The dermatologist said, "Use baking soda or corn starch to keep it dry – and wait two weeks." I had a similar encounter when I was 35 years old.

When our son, Walt, was nine, he took off his shirt while helping Chub clear a fence row. He was literally covered with the rash, but somehow Chub was not affected. After that, we all used "liquid glove," a product made for mechanics and painters. And we really respected those "leaves three."

Years later Walt had it in his beard one Christmas week. Poison ivy rash in winter was new to us. The doctor explained that he probably contacted it on firewood – or even walking in the smoke from firewood on which ivy grew. He had seen patients whose rash came from pets and from car fenders that brushed the ivy or from shoes they had worn in the woods. He advised, "Leaves three? Turn and flee."

Poison ivy clings to trees, grows on the ground or in ditches and places where little else survives. The oil is found in all parts of the plant all year long. After spending time in the woods, it's a good idea to scrub exposed parts with cool water and strong soap. Drop outer clothing in the washer and remember to remove the oil that is probably on the shoes you wore. The five leaves of Virginia Creeper and woodbine are harmless. "Leaves five, let it thrive." As for three leaves? Flee! But watch where you're stepping!

In 1960 we camped in Newfoundland and the kids pumped "to fill up the lake." Walt's pants never stayed up when he was busy.

My covered wagon folk sculpture, made of local clay.

SPRINGS AND MUD HOLES
ARE FOREVER

When my friend Mary Grace heard that we'd bought the Chris Baumgartner place, she said, "Oh, you own that wonderful spring!" She lived a mile south, as the crow flies, and she said that people depended on that water in the dry years of the 30s. "Otherwise they'd have had to sell their animals and possibly lose their farms," she said. "People from all around came with teams and wagons and filled their barrels and they never dipped that spring dry."

Springs are sources of good water where it flows through the earth. Consider the importance of pure water to a family crossing central Missouri in a covered wagon. Frontiersmen pushed westward through Missouri around 1800, their wagons following Indian paths. Indians used springs, which are often located in valleys or on hillsides. Water, which falls as rain, travels through porous rock or under impervious rock or clay, sometimes for many miles. When it "outcrops" to the surface, earth-cooled water can be collected by digging a hole in the ground and walling it with stones. Mary Grace said the spring on our place was "in a low place between a hill and the site of the old road." I recalled her words many years later.

One summer day when I was wandering in that general area of our farm, I thought about the spring and explored where wild roses, blackberry bushes and poison ivy were exceptionally lush and green. The surrounding trees were too. I worked my way through the briars, detouring around the ivy, and reached the middle of this tangle. It was an oasis of healthy growth and in the middle was a big depression in the ground. Poison ivy almost obscured the huge limestone rocks encircling the hole. Eureka! I found it!

I took my bearings so I'd be able to find it again. I identified the old gravel road site covered with sod but with no trees or briars or bushes. The spring was near the place where wagons and buggies once crossed the creek on wide, flat layers of solid limestone rocks. We've had many a picnic on those rocks, but the briars and ivy had turned us back from the area of the spring.

Later I chopped a path through the wild roses and blackberries but detoured around poison ivy. I sprayed ivy that grew inside the spring's wall and later raked out leaves and trash as far as I could reach. Poking the rake handle farther down, it came out clean and wet! The ground water was still there.

We never completed cleaning it out, but several years ago my grandchildren and I showed this spring to a fellow who understood Indians' living habits. He explained that Indians probably had used water from this spring two or three hundred years before Europeans came.

A similar outcropping had been walled up on Columbia's eastern slope early in the 1800s. Old maps showed the location of springs to help pioneers visit these sources of water for themselves and their animals as they extended the frontier westward. When covered wagons were known to be on the Boone's Lick Trail approaching Columbia, men hitched up their teams and went to help the ox teams pull their wagons through mud holes. The first *Atlas of Boone County*, issued in 1876, showed the existence of springs on Hospital Hill and a street named Spring Street, between present-day Walnut and Broadway. The spring for which Spring Street was named is still there with water seeping out as it did 200 years ago. Spring Street is now the private driveway through Boone Medical Park. A workman told me, "We all know about that spring. Our equipment kept getting stuck in the mud when the park was under construction."

Local history refers to the helpfulness of Columbia residents this way: When word reached downtown Columbia that there were wagons on the Boone's Lick Trail, men hitched up their mule teams and went to help the travelers through the mud. In 1979 I used local white clay to represent just such a situation. The 54-inch folk sculpture is mounted in the admissions lobby of Boone Hospital Center, across the street from the spring and the mud.

Yes, springs and mud must go on forever!

Walt's eighth birthday cake was a ball and catcher's mitt.

AIRPLANE CAKE

MAY 18, 1958

Walt was too sick to open his presents – two weeks ago measles hit the school and hit his room hardest of all. There were more empty desks facing Mrs. Moreau this week than ones that were occupied. Walt was up early but not bright, for this was his bad day.

The doctor says a typical pattern is for a youngster to be feverish and weary the first day with cough developing. Then the fever subsides a bit and the cough continues for a couple of days. Walt even felt good during these in-between days, but we knew it was measles because Nancy had been through the similar stages four days ago. She's feeling almost like a human being today.

After breakfast Walt had an aspirin and managed to prop his eyelids open long enough to undo the packages to discover a football, hammer and wire pliers, his first real fly line and some other tackle including Chub's old automatic reel and my rebuilt fly rod. For a seven-year-old, he's remarkably successful with a fly rod and has used a borrowed one enough to demonstrate that he can take care of it.

We have a habit of making a birthday cake in some interesting and unusual shape. I had planned to make a "fish" cake this year, but Walt said, "I really wanted it to be an airplane." So, with his promise not to be disappointed if it flopped, I set about—with two too many helpers—to make an airplane. Cardboard wings were iced to match the fuselage. Motors and other attachments were of candy bars and chocolate drops. Actually, it looked like a plane to Walt because he had thought of it and had located a photo of a World War II model to copy, and because he helped mix the icing until he could hold his head up no longer. I was happy to cut the thing and eat it, lest someone drop in and say, "What in the world is THAT?"

In spite of everything, it was a very good cake, but I'll never try to carve a difficult shape out of sponge cake again. I usually use loaf angel food cake that's about two days old and it responds nicely to the carving knife. It tastes good too, especially when shaped into a colorful railroad train or a tractor and wagon loaded with angel food hay bales or a catcher's mitt.

At bedtime, I realized that nobody had even suggested spanking our "measly" birthday boy, and he turned for me to do the job. It was hard to spank those seven whops and one to grow on, but he wanted it because that made it really seem like a birthday. I sure hope he has no more returns of this day.

COUNTRY ROAD

When we leave the state blacktop highway on our way home, we're still four miles away and it's mostly gravel. Our Vemer's Ford Road is a one lane, winding tunnel of trees. At dusk today the fragrance of wild cherry blossoms make this trip special. I slow to a stop on Blue Hill to look for the foliage of the wild flowers that gave the hill its name. With a glance in the mirror, I get out for a moment, but bluebell foliage is soon gone after the flowers shatter. Next spring before the buds show up, I'll move some more from the woods. Honeybees make a faint humming sound as they pour from the sky to the landing board and wobble into the hive, some with loaded pollen baskets heavy on their legs.

Whip-poor-wills come out of the woods on spring nights like this and sit in the roadway looking like a clump of mud. Rabbits come out into the warm roadbed to dry off after a sudden shower, but not this evening. In winter the birds line up in the tracks where tires have cut through light snow. They peck at bits of the sand that birds need in their gizzards for grinding seeds.

Farther on I see a fox, a red one. He is on his way somewhere, his plume of tail sticking straight out behind and is gone by the time I identify him. It's unusual to see a gray fox in this part of the country.

Deer in the road become confused when blinded by headlights and are likely to bolt into the woods without looking. One broke his neck doing that last winter. He rammed into a fence that he didn't see. Most often they dart out of the woods and leap, fairly floating though the air with the white underpart of the tail unfurled like a flag.

Actually, it's the lowly spider webs that make our dead end road so special. At night they cast their webs all the way across the lane. Those are gossamer gates we never want to open. We have counted as many as fourteen rabbits between the bigger gravel road and the entrance to our driveway and as many as six squirrels.

The most unusual creatures we have seen—and I've seen them twice—were the two ringtail wildcats we saw at the Bennett's driveway. I was alone the first time and Chub and I saw them about a year later. Any season of the year, the drive from the state road to our mailbox is certain to have some creature surprises.

TIGER HUNT

In 1987 my three little grandsons were staring with blank faces at the television screen that was jiggling and dancing with play-like creatures that performed impossible feats, brutal acts of destruction and a few acts of kindness. I have noticed that there are hours of this kind of screeching and screaming in high-pitched, falsetto voices. The action bounces rapid-fire so there's no time for the viewer to wonder if it's more exciting on the other channel.

So I spoke to my three grandsons. The ad man was selling something which kids "have to have" if they ever hope to be <u>anybody</u>. These kids wanted to buy whatever it was. Our Nancy and Walt once fell in love with a "Webster Spiral Blade" and wanted that for Christmas—more than any other thing. It was for a carpenter, not for kids. They got it, along with kid gifts, and we never heard another word about spiral blades!

Almost nobody advertises good old cooked cereal or fresh spinach or soap and warm water on a washcloth! I felt pressed to stage an act that would rival the endless Saturday morning intoxication. I felt I had to sing and dance and stand on my head to compete with such hullabaloo. And I'm a 73-year-old grandmother!

Old or not, I'm a daring competitor. My first attempt was a disaster. When I suggested that we turn off the programs, they chorused, "There's nothing else to do!"

"Think of something, Granny!" I said to myself.

"Well, we could go on a tiger hunt," I offered, as if that were a normal thing to do on our mid-Missouri farm.

"For a real tiger?" Oliver asked, with wide sparkling black eyes.

"I haven't seen one recently, but I've seen some big tracks on the muddy creek bank—too big for a raccoon or a possum."

"Which creek bank?" Peter asked, rolling over on his back. I was making headway!

"You'll see," I replied with Granny's old standby.

"You're kidding, Granny?" eight-year-old Cole asked with twinkling eyes.

"You'll see," I said again, twinkling my eyes back at him.

We chose backpacks for all. Everybody carried a bottle of cold water, a box of raisins and an orange. Then we put a small, empty container into each pack, "Who knows what you'll want to bring from Tiger Country?" Cole carried a pocket knife, Peter the first-aid kit and Oliver a referee's whistle, in case the rest of us got lost from him. We loaded into the van because I didn't want us to have to climb the hill coming home.

I parked at the side of our lane near where a little branch of a creek flows under the road through a big culvert. We un-loaded, put on the backpacks and I ordered, "Stop! Which one of these plants is poison ivy?" Cole recognized it and we detoured around it chanting, "Leaves Three, Turn and Flee."

Seat-scooting down a clay bank by digging our heels in and holding to brush and roots, no one tumbled down too fast. Oliver rejected my offer to help and said, "I can do it by myself." He did, of course. I like that attitude and told him so.

"Hey! <u>Real</u> sand," Cole yelled from up ahead. Oliver and Peter joined him and they made castles with dungeons and tunnels galore. Pete discovered some tracks and all three followed along the creek bank finding places where raccoons had washed their food. Lacy bird tracks decorated the mud at water's edge. Where there was a larger hole of water, we identified deer tracks by the divided, double-hoof prints.

"See any tiger tracks yet?" I said when the boys raced ahead of me.

They'd forgotten that this was a tiger hunt. "Not yet, but here are some itty bitty fish in this puddle." To my surprise, Cole soon stood up with a tiny minnow in his hand. It wasn't an inch long! "Granny, can I keep him? He'll die in this little puddle."

I quickly produced a paper cup, dipped up some creek water, and he dropped in his tiny fish. Cole was proud and I was surprised that he actually caught one in his hands. He released it into a bigger water hole when we found one.

"Everybody over here!" Pete called, motioning to the rest of us. "Here are some really BIG tracks."

"Tigers?" I asked.

"Now, Granny ..." He gave me a look of you-know-better-than-that.

Cole and Oliver ran to see the really big tracks. They guessed a lot and finally agreed that a big dog had made them.

It was past lunch time so we ate the oranges and they

explored without supervision. I said, "I'll be waiting in the van. When you hear me honk a long and two shorts, you must come running."

For about 15 minutes, I pondered the events of the morning. The TV ads, the concentration, the screeching wheels and exploding buildings. ... How will Oliver, Peter and Cole be able to sort out what's true? Sand is "real" when water put it there. Wiggly fish in a paper cup are real. Mud is, poison ivy is, and being alone in the woods is good practice for things to come. I didn't know then that Cole would earn high school letters in wrestling and a scholarship to New York University. I couldn't predict that Peter would be my mainstay computer instructor who wants to go to MIT after high school. I never dreamed that Oliver would win a wrestling medal in his very first tournament and would enjoy writing stories.

I did know, however, that this Tiger Hunt was helping them sort out what's real, what's true. And I'm still happy about that.

I honked and they came running. Nobody was disappointed about not encountering a real tiger. As they scraped mud off their shoes, we agreed that we never go to the woods without finding something interesting to do.

Yes, there <u>are</u> other things to do on a Saturday morning! ✍

STRANGE HAPPENING
IN THE SKY

It's exactly 45 stride steps from the carport to my pottery
workshop and at exactly 6 a.m. on a dark November morning in
1989 I tiptoed past the dog house. I didn't want to wake Rosie
because she might bound out of her bed and cause me to drop
the tray of fragile clay sculptures I was carrying. On the way to
my workshop, I hesitated, enjoying the bright stars. I recalled
my childhood belief that stars were tiny peep holes into heaven.
Suddenly I gasped! The whole northern sky was aglow. My
first thought was that all of Centralia was on fire. No, it was a
beautiful green, pink and lavender with vertical gray streaks.

I hadn't seen such a display in decades. "Northern lights,"
we called them because we couldn't pronounce "aurora borealis." Several times in my childhood, Mom woke us to go outdoors and see the beautiful display. Later she taught us to say,
"aurora borealis." We saw them in late summer and I assumed
that this sky show was associated with hot summer nights. I
took the tray of fragile sculpture pieces to the workshop and
glanced at the clock.

Then I hurried up the pond bank for a better view. There

was a slow, gentle rolling movement as many colors smeared across the wide black backdrop. Should I wake Chub? No. As a child, I once ran to the barn where Dad was milking and told him we were watching the Northern lights. He said, "Oh?" and kept on milking. This morning I stood there, etching the view into my memory.

Rosie pawed my leg to get attention. I rubbed her head and, without taking my eyes off the sky, told her that she might never see an aurora borealis again. The vertical streaks seemed to melt into the colorful glow. I was surprised that there was no reflection of this in the calm pond water. Perhaps that relates to the fact that this natural occurrence is caused by electrically charged particles from the sun—and it's 60 to 600 miles above the earth.

The displays I saw as a child looked more like a stack of flattened rainbows following the contour of the horizon. I told Mom it looked like the beautiful fan of feathers of some gigantic turkey gobbler. She said, "Northern lights happen only when everything is just right." I didn't know what that meant but if Mom said it, it was so.

This was not like I remembered, but I suspect that no two aurora displays are alike. Why hadn't I run for the camera? The colors disappeared quickly and the black curtain turned to gray. The sun wasn't yet in sight as I went into the workshop at exactly 6:30 a.m.

I called to share this experience with my 10-year-old grandson Sam Russell. It was get-ready-for-school time so I hurriedly said, "I've just seen the most beautiful sight in the sky. Your mother can help you learn to say aurora borealis and it means Northern..."

He interrupted me. "Oh, yeah, I know all about aurora borealis. There's this legend. Aurora was the Roman goddess of dawn who opened the gates of heaven each morning to let the sun god drive across the sky."

"Oh?" I said, stunned.

"Yeah, she didn't like her lover when he got old so she turned him into a grasshopper."

Gee, thanks, Sam!

DO YOU HEAR THE NOISES OF CORN?

Do you listen to the noises that corn makes...
The crackling as seed splatters into planter boxes...

The clatter of plates dealing grains into moist earth...
The gentle whisper of newborn leaves in their first breeze?

The caressing of thankful blades on cultivator fenders...
The limp tassels begging cloudless skies for moisture...

The melody of raindrops resuscitating thirsty plants...
The silence? And do you smell the musty fragrance...

Of pollen drifting
                    down,
                          into hollow
                                      silk tubes,
Piping life stuff to every grain-to-be?

Do you hear dry leaves chattering in September...
The clacking of grains spilling into sheller hoppers...

Grinder burrs releasing flavor
For animals and for you and me?

Are you listening? Do you hear...
Corn seed splattering into other planter boxes?

I listen. I hear.
I like the noises that corn makes!

MY SLING SHOT

City influence crept into our country life this week as we walked, dream-shopping, through a toy store. I was appalled when Nancy began begging to BUY a sling shot. My shock was not because of the begging but the buying! Now to me, buying a sling shot is sacrilege—unheard of—ridiculous! The very thought of a sling shot, machine-made of smoothly polished oak with rounded "V", beveled edges made my skin crawl. That was the payoff. Even the 49 cents didn't make me see red. It was the thought of this "younger generation" having to have things made for them, things that were handed over finished and ready to use.

I was reminded of my own childhood when the doing was more important than the having. In the case of a sling shot, the making was always more fun than the shooting. I'd hunt for days for the perfect green, forked stick that fit my palm just right. Then I'd peel the bark off and feel the smooth, slimy new wood in my grip. The cut ends would be whittled smooth and the grooves cut so the rubber sling could be attached to the arms of the "Y." Dad saved old inner tubes for me just for this purpose. I liked the red ones best because they looked the prettiest. I sometimes sneaked Mom's best dressmaking scissors out to cut the strips. Rounding the edges of the rubber was important to make the sling shot "neat." I discovered that an old leather shoe tongue made just the right ammunition holder and I'd lace it together with infinite care. When I was finished and had zinged a few pebbles at non-moving targets, I started looking for an even more perfect forked stick for my next sling shot. Maybe a bigger one would make the barn roof clang a little louder?

I guess that's what the philosopher meant when he said, "It is better to travel hopefully than to arrive."

THIRSTY COWS

Creeks and ponds were frozen over and neither the cows nor the two horses could get water. Sometimes cows can lick through the ice and horses can paw through it, but not on this day. It was eight degrees below zero! Chub was at work and I was to cut holes in the pond ice when the cows needed water, which was usually about noon.

I bundled up so the frozen particles in the air couldn't touch any place except my eyes and walked sideways, a large double-bladed ax resting on one shoulder. Fuey, our Pekingese, loped through the deep snow and loved it. Soon 35 Shorthorns came out of the timber and followed us to the pond west of the house. Sharp splinters of ice struck me as I began to chop. I loosened the scarf around my face as I rested. I had chopped four inches in one spot and no water oozed out in sight.

The thirsty animals crowded around me, some of their faces were right down where I was chopping. I wondered how 35 cows would take turns if I ever chopped through to water. I turned and threatened them to get them to move back so I could swing that double-bladed ax. The ice was at least six inches deep and it gripped the ax when I finally saw water. All of the cows wanted it at once. I continued to frighten them away and whittle away at the ice. The ax was heavier with every blow as the water froze on it instantly. Water also froze on my boots, pants legs and gloves.

Finally I had a hole about a foot square and the cows knew it! The chunk of ice covering the hole, however, had to be removed before any of them could drink. By turning the ax sideways, I tilted the ice enough to get the ax under one edge and finally got one corner out of the hole. After several attempts, the entire chunk was out of the way. I was too! The two most aggressive cows drank at the same time and others tried, unsuccessfully, to push them aside.

Of course I was soon chopping a second hole. It was easier because the cows ignored my chopping in favor of pushing forward to the open water. My frozen pants legs were pulled down over the five-buckle overshoes so the ice didn't touch my legs. Icy gloves kept the cold from reaching my hands. I went to the house with a warm, satisfied feeling. Oh, the music of thirsty cattle slurping water!

Each morning I read, on my refrigerator door, "Pure joy comes ... from doing something worthwhile." I'm joyful today!

NOT ALL PROFIT

Nancy was about ten when she assumed the responsibility of one hive of honey bees. Chub was the beekeeper at that time, but not for long. They were installing a queen in Nancy's hive one day and the hive was open. Just as they were lighting the dry leaves in the bee smoker, big drops of rain splattered down into the open hive and the bees went after Nancy. She got several stings on her face before the event ended.

The next day both of her eyes were swollen shut. We were expecting Maxine Lincoln and Jean Cronan and their children for a visit the next afternoon. Nancy could barely see by holding her head a certain way and she was mortified that Mike Cronan would see her like this.

"Honey, would you like to sell your bees to me?" I asked.

She quickly said, "No!" After thinking it over she said, "This just proves that it's not all profit." We're often reminded that nothing is all profit in this business of farming.

In September, 1973, Chub was in Kansas City, Nancy was married and Walt owned the bike shop and lived at home. While I was talking on the telephone, I was idly looking out the window. "You should see the seven jars of warm elderberry jelly on my cabinet," I said. Then I interrupted the conversation, saying, "I must hang up, there's something wrong with a big steer over in the far pasture."

I drove the pickup across the branch and to the west pasture for a closer look. A steer of about 300 pounds was bawling and going around in circles and it seemed that something was covering his face. Sure enough, there was a tall metal bucket on his face with the bail hooked over the back of his head. He couldn't see or eat or drink.

Nancy called her husband Mike, and I called Walt at his shop. The steer's hip bones stuck out over the sunken places below. He obviously needed water; however, he certainly had plenty of energy! Mike and Walt got a lasso and the bolt cutters and the three of us hurried to the pasture in the pickup. Suddenly it started to rain hard. I watched from the truck as the boys drove the big calf into a fence corner. Walt failed when he tried to throw his lasso over the steer's head. Mike teased him for missing. The rain came harder than ever.

When the steer bounded into the fence, Mike caught hold of the bucket and wrestled him around but finally lost his grip and the steer took off down the fence, bellowing into the bucket with every breath. These non-cowboys laughed and yelled, teasing each other, as the poor steer ran back and forth in the cloudburst. The fellows were soaked to the skin. Walt caught hold of the bucket and began to wrestle. He yanked in one direction just as the steer turned the other. Off came the bucket! Everybody screamed with joy and the surprised steer trotted off to look for food and water.

The cattle business, like beekeeping, isn't all profit!

GRANNY LOOKS BACK

Cole, Peter, and Oliver (from left) brought nineteen toads to show what they caught in the dry swimming pool.

DAD, MOM
AND OLD CICERO

As a green freshman at MU in 1932, I was required to take science, English, history, government—core subjects for first-year students. To liven up that schedule, I chose "Cicero's Essays" as an elective. I felt quite comfortable with Old Cicero. After four years of Latin at University High School, we were well past the "amo, amas, amat" stage and had begun to appreciate what those old Romans were trying to say to their contemporaries and to us. Dad and Mom were trying to say the same things to my brother and me.

Dad's formal education was in a one-room country school. Mom completed high school. The rest of their learning came from reading and from life experiences. Cicero said that "friendship is genuine and spontaneous," and "nothing is feigned or pretended." Mom and Dad said it this way, "A friend in need is a friend indeed."

Cicero wrote at length about old age and friendship. I have a sweatshirt that declares, "THE OLDER, THE WISER." Indians and early Boone County settlers said, "Young men are for war, old men are for wisdom." Being old, however, does not guarantee wisdom.

Our parents selected our playmates because farmers lived too far apart to have many drop-in friends. If I asked, "Can Catherine come over to play?" that meant that her mother had to hitch the little brown pony to the two-person buggy and bring Catherine five miles to our home. Our Mom's spent some afternoons together while we girls were becoming good friends. Both women valued true friendship.

Catherine's mother, Hattie, became the important "third party" in my life. Parents are of first importance, of course, but Catherine's mother was important to me also. She never ceased to learn. Cicero claimed that, "Unless you pour oil into the lamp, the powers of the mind are extinguished by old age." Hattie enrolled in the University School of Journalism at an advanced age. That was her way of "pouring oil in the lamp."

In addition to wisdom, Cicero championed a code of moral behavior which demanded honesty, fairness and truthfulness. Integrity was his theme song! He said, "Integrity augments the resources, even of robbers."

Dad and Mom didn't use the word "integrity," but they knew that a man's word was good as his bond. Farmers bought and sold hay, animals, grain and even property with a handshake. There wasn't any bookkeeping between friends who traded blacksmithing for the use of a team and wagon at thrashing time.

The old philosopher—and early residents in this nation— knew that friendship is genuine, spontaneous and "nothing is feigned, nothing is pretended." It's as true today as it was in Cicero's day—or Dad's.

WHY THE "LICK" IN BOONE'S LICK?

"Ol' Dan'l didn't take much to larnin'." He didn't even spell his name the same every time. So don't be surprised that our section of mid-Missouri was "Boone's Lick Country" and often spelled "Boonslick."

But regardless of the spelling, our land was in a large wilderness called Upper Louisiana (Louisiana Purchase, 1803) which later came to be known as Boone's Lick Country and finally as Boone County, Missouri. Why was Lick a part of that name?

Imagine, if you will, heading into an unknown wilderness with a half dozen cows pulling your homemade wagon—and you with a young spouse and a "passel of young 'uns." You're carrying guns, kettles, bedding, medicine, seeds, and tools enough to build and equip your log home.

You'll kill the game that feeds the hungry family in zero cold. You'll stir the earth so you can plant, nurture and harvest food. The Bible is your library. The mail won't come, the phone won't ring, you'll not need the roto-rooter man!

But you will need salt. Salt will tan the hides, cure the

meat, season the corn meal mush and make the sauerkraut so there'll be a vegetable in your diet in winter.

Daniel Boone's namesake son, Daniel Morgan Boone, (called Morgan) came from Kentucky to Missouri and located a beautiful spot not far west of the Mississippi River—in what is now St. Charles County. After several years of successful hunting in that area, he returned to Kentucky and talked his Dad into moving to this beautiful place. "It's got everything you want," he told his aging father, "clear, flowing rivers and streams, fish, lots of wild game, fertile fields and Indians."

The elder Boone led a group of families to this spot, built a log cabin for Rebecca and their nine children and explored farther west during long hunts. Although Daniel was 65 years old when he made the move, he followed the river into central Missouri's wilderness, hunting and trapping and making friends with the Indians.

A long hunt usually began in early winter when animal fur was thick and beautiful; he was often gone from home two months or more. During such a trip in about 1805, Indians told the famous old hunter how to the locate a large "salt lick."

The licks were important to animals for they needed salt in their diets and they got it by licking the brackish earth around various salt springs. Because salty water had oozed out of the ground for thousands of years, a low mound of salt built up around the springs. Wild animals licked there. What better place for Indians and pioneers to find game?

More important, what better place for frontiersmen to manufacture salt? Young Nathan, ambitious and not afraid of work, needed money because he was building a mansion for his growing family. (His home is now erroneously called "Daniel Boone's

Home.") Salt would sell well at the fur trading post called St. Louis. The brothers went to check out the salt lick in the fall of 1806 and made plans to manufacture salt the following year.

It was not unusual for women like Nathan's wife, Olive, to be left alone for several months to tend the crops, run the household, milk the cows, and walk the floor when children were ill, all the while glancing over their shoulders to see if "my man" might be coming home that day.

The Boone brothers had learned woodsmanship, exploring and surveying from their father. They had learned to make salt back in Kentucky at "Blue Licks." Nathan and Morgan, therefore, brought iron kettles, wagons, oxen and all of the other supplies they needed and traveled the 150 miles to boil salty water and ship the finished product down river to the market. They made buckets, troughs, shovels and other items from the maple, hickory and oak trees in the surrounding woods.

The Boones needed oxen to drag logs to their salt furnace, so they opted to go overland instead of boating down the river. They followed the ridgetops as they blazed a trail from near St. Charles to the salt lick. As other wagons followed their trail, it became the thoroughfare to the West, connecting with the Santa Fe and Oregon Trails. Some settlers stopped along the Boone's Lick Trail, built log cabins on the crest of a hill and called it Smithton. A year and a half later, Smithton was abandoned in favor of a new village down the hill near Flat Branch. That was the beginning of Columbia.

When I was a child, Fulton Gravel (which followed the Boonslick Trail) became the shortest route between New York City and Los Angeles. About 1929 a concrete road called "the Slab" replaced the gravel road. It became Highway 40 and later was improved into I-70. History books record that modern engineers generally followed the route of the Boones across Missouri.

Just how did the Boones get from St. Charles to the salt lick? Get a map of Missouri and locate Nathan's home near Defiance in St. Charles County. Follow I-70 west and locate Boonville, then look northwest to Boonesboro. You'll find "Boone's Lick" and the green triangle indicating a point of interest nearby. It's near a wide place in the Missouri River across from Arrow Rock. Drive there and take your imagination along! 🏺

HARG CROSSROADS

When I was a kid, Mr. William McHarg would unlock his store after church so members of the congregation could exchange eggs, butter and cream for groceries, chicken feed, coal oil or whatever they needed. Many had driven a buggy, surrey or wagon four or more miles to get to church and it was an accommodation to them not to have to make a trip back for things they needed. Mr. William and Cynthia were pillars in Olivet Church.

The church building was on one of the four corners of the crossroads called Harg. McHarg's store, McHarg's home and a blacksmith shop were on the other three. In the early 1900s, Harg was on the most direct route between New York and California and occasionally strangers stopped there to ask directions. Mr. William installed a gas pump and finally, in the late 20s, put in a table and chairs and served homemade pies. One traveler told another until Cynthia and Phanah Grant were kept busy baking those pies.

The store became a center of community activity every day of the week. People picked up the mail there, they met to work out church and community problems, they voted there and, on Saturday nights, men would gather around a table and play "Pitch." There was joking, storytelling and gossip involved, but no gambling.

Lots of customers would have Mr. William "write it down"— they'd pay later, when they could. He financed many an order for which he had no hope of collecting. Some customers would trade wild gooseberries, black walnuts, hickory nuts and sometimes garden produce for coffee, tobacco, salt, sugar and other items which they didn't produce on their farms.

There were wooden benches under the big grape arbor in front of the store; this was a favorite resting place, especially in August when those concord grapes turned purple. And there were hitching racks for those who came on horseback, by buggy, or wagon. The community centered around that church, store, and blacksmith shop which was Harg. It was even on the Missouri road map.

The McHarg family came from Maghera, Ireland, to America in about 1860 and settled on a farm overlooking this country crossroads. The family included three school teachers and two merchants, a carpenter and others. As time passed, the blacksmith shop became a garage and the new highway U.S. 40 left Harg off the map. Old 40 has now been replaced by Interstate 70, a few miles north of the crossroads that was once Harg. 🔔

CAUGHT A BIG ONE

During W.W.II Chub was waiting for reassignment with the Coast Guard and we lived in an apartment at Winthrop Beach, Massachusetts, where our windows overlooked the ocean. During a storm, saltwater sprayed our second floor windows. Fisherman that I claim to be, I was anxious to try my luck in the ocean.

My friend Millie Elliott, a major's wife, said, "I know a place where we can fish from a high crag without poles."

We bought heavy saltwater tackle including coils of stiff line, heavy sinkers and large barbed hooks that would have surrounded a half dollar without touching. Millie said, "I'll put Glen in the movie and we'll take Lucy Cobb with us."

We drove north to Nahant, parked and climbed a long rocky path to the point where we were to fish. The ocean was far below and the waves lashed the vertical rock bluffs. It would take a good throw to get the hooks and sinkers out far enough.

Millie's little girl was no problem at all; she made up some games with her dolls and several tiny rocks. Millie and I rewound the tackle so we could sling the loops out, the way a lifeguard slings a ring buoy. Soon we had a couple of ugly ocean catfish.

Each time I rewound and slung, I was thinking how much this was like throwing a buoy. One time, however, when I let go of the coils, the big hook caught my wool slacks and went into the back of my leg behind my knee. I grabbed the heavy sinker and held it to relieve the pain. Millie turned pale and then white! There I stood, on one leg, my driver about to faint, a tiny little girl to consider and a fish hook buried in my leg. We were miles from any town where we'd find a doctor.

I comforted Millie and said, "Reach into my right side pocket and get my knife to cut off this heavy sinker."

Her color improved a little and I helped her cut off the sinker, rip the seam of the pants and cut the green wool pant leg away except where the hook held it against my flesh. Surprisingly, there was no bleeding and it didn't hurt much because the barb went all of the way through the flesh. We gathered our tackle and lunch stuff, even the three worthless catfish, and walked down the rocky path to the car. I worried more about Millie's being able to drive than about my leg.

It was the doctor's day off so we went to the hospital and a young fellow tried to back the hook out, the barb hurting me a lot. "I've heard that you can cut the barb off," I said,

Without a word, he tried to grind the hook off with a surgical instrument. "Millie has some cutters in her car," I prompted.

Without reply, he sent his nurse to the boiler room for a tool with which he snapped the barb off. He removed the other part and asked for iodine and a Band-Aid, then disappeared. There was no charge! 🦉

BUTCHERING DAY

Butchering was done on a cold winter day when the forecast was for more cold days ahead. Handling the various chores of "working up" a lot of fresh meat required a cold spell because of the lack of refrigeration on farms in the early days. After butchering day the meat had to be cured or canned or fried down to prevent spoilage.

Preparation usually began a few days ahead of the actual hog killin'. Men set the scalding trough in place and split wood for the fires. They brought butchering tables out of the smoke house and scrubbed them. They sharpened axes and knives, scrubbed the sausage grinder and washed several tubs, which would handle hundreds of pounds of fresh pork. A large family would butcher several hogs on butchering day. A small family might bring a hog of their own to be processed along with those of the hosts.

Women prepared ahead too. They gathered the seasoning spices, sewed up long narrow sausage sacks and washed the big stoneware jars for the fried-down sausage. They prepared for a big noon meal and washed and scalded glass canning jars, which were used to "cold pack" the tenderloin. Butchering day was a combination of hard work and a neighborhood social event. A little wine or whiskey helped the men endure the sometimes blizzard conditions of the long, busy day.

There's an art to almost every chore on butchering day. For example, the water in the scalding tub had to be tested by hand. If it was hot enough, the hog's hair would slip just right. If it was too hot, the hair would "set" and be difficult to remove. If the tester streaked his finger through the water two times but couldn't endure the third, then he gave the signal and four or more men lifted the animal into the water. The carcass couldn't be left long in the hot water so the men would stand by and lift it out at just the right time. They'd put the hog on a table and use sharp, stiff knives to scrape the hair off.

The clean, white carcass was then hung upside down on a tall pole frame. A tub below caught the discarded parts, and someone sawed each hanging carcass lengthwise. The men would carry the halves to the tables to be trimmed into hams, shoulders, side slabs and other cuts. The organ meat would go to the kitchen where the women gave them a final cleaning. Some of the livers were soaked in vinegar water and then fried for the noon dinner.

At outdoor tables men trimmed hams and shoulders. Lean scraps were put aside for the sausage grinder. The skin and fat were cut into small chunks and cooked in a big iron kettle to render the lard. This hot liquid grease was strained and the cooked skin that remained, called "cracklin's," were chewy and tasty treats for the people as they worked or used to enhance the flavor of cornbread in winter. The raw lean meat was ground for sausage. The grinder was turned by hand and the pink curls of meat would drop into a tub below. Tubs of sausage were carried into the kitchen after the dinner dishes were put away. Women scrubbed their hands and squeezed the spices into the sausage. Each family has a special recipe for seasoning sausage. Dad got ours from "Old Man Easley," but we put in extra sage because Chub used to say, "It's not sausage without sage."

When the mixing and tasting were complete, the women stuffed the raw, spiced meat into long cotton bags. The spices helped preserve the meat, which was hung in a dry, cool place. Sometimes all or part of the sausage was fried till nearly done and then packed into stoneware jars and sealed with excess grease left from the frying.

At the end of the day, the helpers set a date for butchering at the next farm. Everybody got sausage, organ meat or cracklin's to take home. Hog killin' day was only the beginning; canning lasted for several more days and curing was done later. The meat was rubbed with a mixture of salt, pepper and other ingredients, then kept in a cool place.

Dad and many others had smoke houses where the additional flavor of hickory smoke was added to the meat. Dad put a small corner room in the fieldstone garage he built. He'd hang the cured hams, shoulders and bacon slabs on hooks for a while. Dad then lit a small fire using hickory shavings and kindling. He tended the fire to keep it smoldering for a long time, giving the meat an extra special flavor.

Dad's people were German so we made special things like souse, head meat, liverwurst and other extras that the Meyerses always enjoyed. Today, store checkers stare at me when I pay for pigs' feet and headcheese. 🏺

Dad and Uncle Archie chat before services in the late 1950s.

WONDERFUL, THE COUNTRY CHURCH

1958

In spring it's wasps and oat bugs. In summer it's women fanning restless babies. In fall and winter it's a balky, smoky furnace and a gale whistling under the baseboard in the choir corner.

Today we stepped over McHarg's collie dog, which had stretched out on the rug in the sun at the entrance to the sanctuary. A little late as usual, we were in time to hear the congregation mispronouncing some Old Testament names as they read responsively. A busy farm wife led a lively discussion about the Sunday School lesson until, suddenly, about 50 noisy children came into the room dropping and picking up their story leaflets. They took their places at the front and became quiet.

We sang and prayed and clapped for those who put birthday pennies in the jar for the Orphans' Home. Then came announcements and the benediction, and then 10 minutes of BEDLAM! Men chatted about hog prices, garden progress and the chances of rain. One fellow traded a bull calf to his friend for clover seed. Three women planned the missionary society meet-

ing and others collected money for a spray of flowers for a
bereaved family. In a similar hubbub, four-year-old Walt tugged
on my skirt and asked, "Isn't ANYBODY listening?"

As the organist began the prelude, I took my place in the
choir with the other altos and shifted my chair so I could frown
at Nancy or Walt, if needed. The little children went to the
playroom and one neighbor boy, dressed in a new blue suit with
white shirt and tie, sat alone in the front pew. Two smiling
sopranos slipped off their fashionable pointed-toed shoes and
were noticeably shorter as we stood to sing.

McHarg's dog roused and sauntered down the aisle, as usual,
and plopped down on the deep pile rug in front of the commun-
ion table. He yawned and dropped off to sleep. My childhood
memories flowed fast: the old toll house with its chain across
the road at the corner of the cemetery, the horses at their
hitching posts east of the church, the ornamental iron fencing
and gates, farmers paying their poll tax by doing a day's work
with mule teams and gravel wagons. And so much more.

The clinking of coins in the wicker collection baskets startled
me back to the present. Soon the organist played the chord and
we all stood to sing the Doxology. "Praise God from whom all
blessings flow..." The little boy on the front row was keeping
time with his pants zipper! Down, up, down, up—he didn't
miss a beat. There were a few anxious moments until we got to
the last ... "Ho-ly Ghost." Down, up, down, UP!

The preacher probably had an inspiring sermon this morning, but wonderful memories crowded all else out this day!

DUDE AND COOT
WERE POLES APART

Orlando Denver and Jesse Hugo were Meyers brothers, born in the late 1800s. They were fondly nicknamed "Dude" and "Coot" by the four half-sisters who raised them. Dude was four years old and Coot was newborn when their mother died. These little fellows were constant companions living on a farm in Lincoln County, Missouri. When Susie, Edie, Mayme and Rose went to their one-room school, they took the boys along when their father and older brother were busy in planting or harvesting.

Dude was O.D. Meyers, my Dad. Coot was my Uncle Jess whom I knew by hearsay and by one photograph. The studio picture in front of a backdrop showed eight or nine young fellows, a group of "rounders." All of them were "gussied up" like gamblers. They wore derby hats at a cocky angle, white shirts, small black ties with dark vests and pants—no coats— and each fellow held an open beer bottle. They were teenagers making a statement; their smiling faces suggesting rebellion. Dad and Uncle Jess had center spots on the front row. Were they gamblers? Maybe. Some said that Coot could make dice obey his commands and could deal cards with sleight of hand that was uncanny.

Dude and Coot felt that they were imposed upon—working hard in the fields for almost no pay. They were bitter about being slaves for their brother and father. This problem was solved when the brother left the farm and their father took Dude in as a partner. The younger Coot skipped out, heading West. He became a mechanic, bought a garage in Yuma, Arizona, and began to market his skill with dice and playing cards.

About 1930 he and his wife made a surprise trip to Missouri to see Dad. The brothers talked till late at night, catching up after so many years apart. Jess had sold the garage, moved to San Diego and was making big money working in gambling houses just across the border in Tia Juana, Mexico. He and Aunt Gladys were fashionably dressed, driving a new car, spending money freely. We all truly enjoyed these "filthy rich" relatives.

He showed us a few tricks of his trade. He accurately predicted how the rolling dice would land. He dealt from the top, bottom or middle of the card deck and told us, as he shuffled the deck, who would get the good poker hand. He put a pile of poker chips on the table and said, "Dude won this pile." He shoved the pile to Dad and we waited. Finally he opened his hands and revealed the high value chips which he "palmed" and said, "I have to use an adhesive when palming silver dollars." How different these brothers were! Mom and Dad, in apron and overalls, worked long hours for little profit. Both families were successful and very happy.

Mom and Aunt Gladys arranged for a Sunday carry-in dinner at Aunt Mayme's home. The four half sisters and their families were there. Jess, the center of attraction, told some stories, embarrassing the women who "mothered" him from birth.

Did Uncle Jess keep the money he palmed? No. Did he gamble? Absolutely not! He was working for the house, employed to make money for the house. He felt that he was making an honest living, marketing his skill for his employers.

"Fools and their money are soon parted," Jess said. "It's my job to help them in the parting process." Then he looked at my teenage brother and said, "Don't ever get the idea that you can get something for nothing. You can't. Nobody can!"

Coot and Dude, from left.

Cole, Peter, and Oliver at the crossing.

FISHING WITH TWO POLES

Sam and Cole were 14 and 16 months old when I first put poles in their hands—small sticks, kind of "play like" fishing poles, that is. Oh, we didn't catch anything that year but that didn't matter. We just pretended that we were fishing and that mattered.

I'd load them into their antique stake-bed farm wagon, like the one I used to dream about and didn't have. I'd pull them down our long driveway to where the water ran across a concrete slab from the cow pasture. We'd throw gravel in the water to hear it go "plunk."

Sometimes we'd float our boats (sticks and leaves) and watch them go over the eight-inch waterfall. They'd disappear under the water only to reappear in some surprising place where the current had taken them. We'd get longer sticks and beat the water to see it splash and to be splashed ourselves sometimes.

"Guys," I said one day, "I'm fishing." That started it.

We'd hold a stick—just any old stick—and wait for a bite. Then we'd pull out an imaginary fish and I'd yell, "Meat on the table!" or "That's a whopper!" or "Get the camera!" Sometimes an imaginary fish got away but we'd always say, "Get him again!" They loved it, especially about the "whopper," even though they couldn't pronounce the word.

We talked a lot about not falling in, about how fishermen need a lifeguard just like swimmers do and about not scaring the fish by beating the water with the stick. We'd usually do that, though, after "fishing."

I'd hold to their shirttails and say, "Back up fellows. You might fall in." The little waterfall had carved out a pool that was about a foot deep. They knew what "fall in" meant, sort of, because we played a lot in their plastic wading pool, but Grannys hold to shirttails, anyway. We made a game out of getting back up the hill. When Peter and Oliver came along a few years later, the "big boys" pushed the wagon and I pulled.

Who needs Saturday cartoons—except on scorching hot afternoons? Fishing in the creek, imaginary tigers, or roasting wieners on Granny's "desert island" was next-to-nature fun.

MY TRANQUILIZERS

Life's minor abrasions and its major frustrations, too, would be hard to take except for my own special-formula tranquilizers. They're free for the seeking and they're a sure cure for the rat race.

When Chub gets poison ivy or mice move into the house for the winter or the washing machine coughs its last or the milk cow cuts jagged lacerations as she pushes through a barbed wire fence—then my tranquilizers see me through.

I smooth out the rough places by grabbing a hoe and chopping buckbrush sprouts out of the asparagus bed. Or I stroll down a woodsy path right after a rain, inhaling the wonderful fragrance of moss and rotted leaves.

Donning boots, I like to tramp through dew-covered pastures where spider webs tie tall weeds together, after daylight and before sunup. Or on an August day, I like taking little Walt for a walk along a dusty cow path, watching the fountains of dust plop up between his bare toes.

Nancy and I like to follow a line of rabbit tracks through new fallen snow until we find a little fellow backed up under a rock ledge or a brush pile. In summer we crunch the mud cracks in a dry creek bed and wonder where the crawdads and tadpoles went—and if they went in time.

It doesn't take much time out of a busy day just to stop and watch a tumble bug roll her lump of manure into a great ball and then push it around in the dust, getting her precious egg that's inside ready for other tumble bugs to take her place in the world.

The children had a favorite place to play under some low branches of hickory trees, at the edge of a field where Chub was planting corn. They called it their camp and begged me to go there with them. I was in a hurry and said, "OK, we'll drive over on our way to town this afternoon."

"Drive!" Walt shouted. "You can't drive to the camp, you... you'd... you'd get there too fast!"

That was the day I learned to take time for tranquilizing, for getting all my senses synchronized. We mustn't get where we're going too fast. So we walked to their camp.

Life will continue to have its minor abrasions, but I have yet to swallow my first tranquilizing pill. My homemade formula continues to work quite well. 🐞

"THE SLAB"

A favorite way to spend Sunday afternoon in the late 20's was to drive over to see the progress on pouring "the slab" that was later named Highway 40, then I-70. We went by Model "T" as we had both a truck and a car by that time. The dairy "T" was a brand new one bought in 1916. A slab road was not needed that early—nor was it even dreamed that there would be that much concrete in the whole world!

Sometimes we went when men and machines were working and we marveled at how far the slab had stretched since the previous visit. I was too young to care about how the sand and gravel and cement were being mixed. The only way I knew to do this was with a mortar box and shovel; however, an endless ribbon of concrete came oozing out of the front of a machine that crept along at a snail's pace. It reminded me of a baby rejecting his cereal by just closing his mouth on it.

This cross-country slab followed close to the old road called Fulton Gravel. I learned to ride my new bike on that road by dodging the bigger rocks of its creek-gravel surface. It had been graveled by local men who used their own shovels, teams and gravel wagons. Some worked out their "poll tax" and others worked by the day for wages. The poll tax was two dollars and a man with team earned two dollars for a day's work; without the team, he earned one dollar.

Just about every farmer had a gravel wagon. Dad's was for keeping our half-mile driveway passable at all times of the year. He had to deliver milk to homes all over Columbia, seven days a week, so he also helped fill mud holes in Fulton Gravel. He shoveled creek gravel into the wagon and filled mud holes in the barn lot, in front of the shed that housed the truck and even at the back of the barn in the "loafing shed" where cows stood waiting to be let in for milking.

The gravel wagon had low sides and a removable bottom made of about eight or ten two-by-fours. The ends of these boards had shaped handles to make it possible to release the gravel directly over the mud holes, without scooping it out of the wagon. The handle shape allowed the hauler to dump the gravel a little at a time. Dad would begin by loosening one two-by-four, which was really hard to get out because of the weight of the gravel. He'd finally shake it loose and the gravel sifted down through the narrow slot. When there was sufficient gravel on the road, he'd urge the mules farther forward and remove other boards until all the gravel was in the mud holes.

That modern road-building machine discharging an endless ribbon of concrete was something worth seeing! How else could they have made a two-lane highway from New York to Los Angeles? Fulton Gravel, now Route WW, was the shortest route across the country even before "the slab" was begun. With mule teams, however, they'd still be shaking gravel out of wagons.

FROSTY,
THE NO-SNOWMAN

Many of the students in my Recreational Leadership class at Christian College were from Kentucky, Texas and Oklahoma. They'd never skated on ice, slid on a snowy hill or made a snowman.

One of their first assignments was to build a snowman, whenever the snow was just right. "Just right" meant that if you squeezed a handful it would stick together and if you rolled a little ball it would pick up snow and soon become a huge ball. I made the assignment in September and students were advised to work in small groups. "Can our boy friends help?" they'd ask.

"Of course," I said, "but you're to help with the project from start to finish."

Sometimes the campus was dotted with snow people because others saw them having fun and went out to do the same. I graded their projects by photo and by what they told me about the experience.

In the late 1940s I came up with a way to make a snowman without snow. It was done with fruit baskets, an old sweat shirt, rag bag sheets or draperies, crumpled newspapers and plaster. We made one on back campus a few years later.

I took a tarp to put underneath "Frosty" to catch the white plaster we'd be splashing and brushing on. We used a bushel apple basket, upside down, for the bottom "snowball" and a half-bushel basket for the torso. A stuffed brown paper bag served as the head. Then we pinned and stitched an old drapery around the large basket and the girls stuffed crumpled newspapers to round it to snowball size and shape. They stuffed the extra cloth underneath the large basket, the sweatshirt over the smaller basket and tied the sleeves together in front and stuffed them. One student read the instructions for mixing plaster to the class. One made a pipe by putting a black cork on a stick. Two created a top hat using a cardboard circle and half of a rolled oats box painted black. Black walnuts were used for buttons and eyes, a carrot for the nose. Someone brought a big red plastic bow and hat band. The men from the shop were interested and brought us an old broom.

We used a throwaway bucket and a wooden spoon for mixing the plaster. Plaster firms up quickly when proper portions are put into water. We used rubber gloves and the girls and I covered the "no-snowman" with plaster by splashing it on with our hands. They mixed and applied until a firm crust developed. They carefully brushed wet plaster on the paper head and let it set up before adding more. Then it was finally time for the top hat. They stuffed thick moist plaster in at the neck, to hold the head upright, tied the red bow in place and stuck the broom under Frosty's arm before it set completely.

We folded the tarp so the splattered plaster didn't show and Frosty stood there, to the wonderment of all, until sometime in

March. The college workmen set him onto the back of my pickup truck and we stored him behind the barn. A quick splashing of fresh plaster was all he needed when Chub brought him from his summer hiding place the next winter.

One year we converted Frosty into the Easter Bunny by making cloth-covered, coat-hanger ears and replacing the broom with a large Easter basket. When our children were old enough to help, we made "Frostys" as Christmas gifts for friends and had to use plastic buckets because we ran out of baskets. Making Frosty was always more fun than just having him! 🐿

Nancy and Walt stuffing Frosty, left. Frosty and me, right.

SMALL WORLD

Susie Mayse and I were idly visiting when she mentioned that she and her husband, Mal, had spent their honeymoon at her grandmother's cabin in Michigan. "Where in Michigan?" I asked.

"Coldwater," she answered. I had spent two weeks in Coldwater, Michigan over 70 years ago.

"I was only 14 years old," I said, "and my friend's father had taught in summer school. He was driving to Coldwater for a short vacation and to accompany the family back to Columbia."

"Oh?" Susie said.

"I went up with Professor Kempster when he..."

"KEMPSTER!," she screamed. "That's who Grandmother bought the cottage from."

Later when Mal Mayse was restoring an old green table from the Michigan property he found "Kempster" written underneath. It must be the same table where we kids made peanut butter and jelly sandwiches in 1928. 🖤

HAYS HARDWARE

In the days when downtown Columbia was all of Columbia, Woolworth's "dime store" and Hays Hardware were on the south side of Broadway, with a small shop in between. Area farm families did most of their shopping, swapping and visiting on Broadway. Any Saturday afternoon they could count on finding their friends congregated on the sidewalk around Woolworth's and Hays Hardware.

After old man Hays died, the store name remained the same. His son, Kirk, took over until his death, and then a nephew, Harold Hickam, inherited the store. Harold's death ended the popular Columbia business.

At least two downtown stores, Miller's Shoe Store and Hays Hardware, had shelves or drawers from floor to ceiling on their walls. In order to get the merchandise down, there was a track near the ceiling and tall wooden ladders on rollers that the clerks used to climb up to get what their customers wanted. The drawers on Hays' wall had little metal pulls on the front and also tags describing their contents. Dad would ask for some special buckle or snap for his mules' harness and the clerk would roll the ladder down to a certain spot and clamor up to the appropriate drawer. Tiny things were in the highest places and big drawers were near the floor. Milk buckets, oil lamps, clocks were kept on shelves.

Larger hardware pieces were stored around the sales room. Oil lanterns hung from the ceiling and could be retrieved with a long pole with a metal hook and knob on the end. Mineral salt blocks were stacked on the floor and harnesses hung in various ways. The leather gave the room a special smell which would shout "Hays Hardware," to even a sightless customer.

People crowded into Woolworth's and Hays on rainy days, but usually "held open house" out on the sidewalk. News was passed from family to family because many had no telephone or daily paper. The raucous laughter and back slapping ended long before sunset. I don't know if Hays had a regular closing time, but farmers in wagons, surreys, buggies and on foot left for home in time to do their chores. Those in cars or trucks also headed home before dark because even gravel roads could be muddy and slippery, and a flat in the dark was no fun.

After the deaths of Harold and Hazel Hickam, the merchandise was sold and Hays Hardware passed from the Columbia scene. Jackie Slater rented the area, complete with roller ladders and a huge old wooden elevator which served three floors. I often sat on that elevator making little clay "people," which Jackie sold in her shop called "Made in Missouri." But when the Woolworth's Store next door burned, the fire damaged the old hardware building enough that it had to be torn down. For those of us who remembered Hays Hardware in its glory days, it was a very sad fire. 🐦

MANUEL'S ICE SKATES

Manuel bought ice skates out of season and resold them in winter by putting a sign in his lawn announcing: "ICE SKATES FOR SALE OR TRADE." After his death, his skates were sold, along with his personal items, at auction on a sultry August day. They were displayed as matched pairs, clean and neatly hanging over a wooden fence. There were hockey skates, racing skates, figure skates, antique skates, new skates still in boxes, skates for all sizes of feet. And there were double-runner skates for tots, old-time Keen Kutter clamp skates and one pair with leather at the heels, like the ones Joe Garity gave me when I was ten years old.

"How much for the skates?" the auctioneer asked. No answer. "How much for choice pair, take as many as you want?" Still no response. "One with the privilege, how much?" Silence. Since these skates had belonged to a relative, I thought it well to start the bidding. "Five dollars."

Nobody else raised that bid so I chose six pairs of various sizes for our grandchildren. The auctioneer chanted on and there were no takers. "Look, folks, I have to sell them. There's all of this other stuff to sell today. How much for the whole batch—all of the ice skates?"

I asked myself, "What in the world would <u>anyone</u> do with all of those skates?"

Pondering that, I recalled that kids outgrow their skates every year and in some winters there's not enough ice to warrant the expense of new skates. Like Manual, I had occasionally bought good skates for a dollar or two per pair, just to lend to guests, friends, 4-H members and others. When ice thickens, my phone rings. "Do you have any skates to fit so and so?" I say, "Come and try them on."

The auctioneer's voice droned on, "Bid something, anything."

Suddenly I heard my weak voice say, "Five dollars." The man pleaded for six, then "SOLD, to Sue Gerard for five dollars!"

Strangers stared, my husband frowned in disgust and friends asked, "What're you going to do with all of those skates, Sue?" I didn't try to answer. Walt drove the pickup truck close to that fence full of skates and began to load my bargain. I counted as Walt and bystanders tossed skates into the truck – 180 pairs of ice skates! It was a rounded pickup load and I have a picture to prove it!

That winter I gave skates to adults and children at Olivet Church, neighbors, friends, Amish children and even 19 pairs to a 4-H group for a garage sale. I had reserved enough to supply our own family as feet grew through the years but there are still about 40 pairs stored away. When winter comes I'll offer the rest to our grandchildren. All seven of them are teenagers needing spending money. Perhaps, like Manuel, they'll put up a sign on a real cold day: "ICE SKATES FOR SALE."

A SMILING
PERFECTIONIST

The first time Eris Lytle saw the stones from St. Mary's Church in London, England, they were a scrambled mess and in America! In addition, they were an ugly black! Luckily, Missouri's winter weather took care of the black which was coal dust from the ship's hold, and the stones were back to normal by spring. Eris didn't know it then, but he faced a challenge no man had ever faced before. He was chosen, by the late John Epple, to be in charge of erecting a London Church on the campus of Westminster College in Fulton, Missouri.

"We don't have any 300-year-old structures in this country," Eris said. "I became obsessed with the church's long history and with Sir Christopher Wren's designs."

The challenge was even greater because every stone had to be placed in the exact row and numbered space in Fulton, as it had been in London. The stones, carefully numbered when they were dismantled from the ruins after WWII, had been hopelessly scrambled during the packing and shipping. This 52-year-old stone mason accepted the tremendous challenge and began supervising the reconstruction.

One workman constantly hunted numbered stones which were spread out on a two-acre lot. Many stones had to be repaired and Eris would cut off the damaged corners and add new ones with stone epoxy. He worked dawn to dusk, to keep the repaired stones ready for placement at the right time.

His wife, Mid, said he'd come home covered with stone dust except for a circular clean spot where his face mask had been. Then he would study the plans far into the night.

Eris is now 94. Friends still enjoy hearing him say, "You start looking for a 4-inch stone that's lost in a 700-ton load; it can be quite a job." John Epple put it this way, "Eris was in charge of solving a gigantic jigsaw puzzle with 7000 pieces."

In 1975 the London Times called Eris Lytle "a smiling perfectionist ... One of the world's leading authorities on architect Sir Christopher Wren ... The man who now knows more about the practicalities of ancient stone masonry than any other American."

WHITE HOUSE COOKBOOK

In about 1973, Nancy and I had a booth at a one-day antique show in the Fayette High School gym. We took turns at the booth and visited around to buy and trade with other dealers. I stopped where a woman was reading a huge cookbook. "Would that be a White House Cook Book?" I asked. The woman flipped it shut so I could see its gleaming white oilcloth cover with big black letters. It had a sunburst circle on the front with a picture of the White House in Washington, DC. I knew that I <u>had</u> to own that book because Mom's copy burned when our house was destroyed by fire in 1922.

The lady opened the front cover and I read, "COMPLI-MENTS of J. L. HENRY, HARDWARE, STOVES, ETC., Centralia, Missouri." I screamed, "That's from Grandpa's store!" Nancy heard me and came running. A few minutes later, Walt appeared at the gym entrance and Nancy yelled for him to come quick. This was a family treasure, for sale to the public. The three of us were making quite a commotion and several people gathered around to see what the racket was about. I held the book tenderly and displayed the first page with its ornamented sticker and said, "That was Mom's father's store in Centralia. This copy was the 1900 edition and Mom would have been a teenage girl." Ida Saxton McKinley's picture was on the front.

The 592 other pages were tan and brittle and I clung to the book so other people wouldn't damage it. This would be our book, whatever the price.

"Mom's White Mountain Cake is in here," I said. Mom made it often. It required the whites of a dozen eggs! It was a four layer cake and she put icing on each layer and held them together with toothpicks. Then she smoothed luscious white icing on the top and sides.

"Once she made it for Tilman Severe's 16th birthday. He was a 16-year-old orphan who came to live with us," I reminisced. These strangers didn't care about Tilman's birthday, but I needed to tell the story. "The icing wouldn't harden and the layers began to slide. We watched her add more toothpicks. But alas, the thing began to split from top to bottom! In desperation she dumped the cake upside down into a huge mixing bowl. "Spoons!" someone yelled and we agreed that there was never a better tasting cake.

I found, "Cakes: Almond ... to ... Variegated" in the loose index pages. There were 76 cake recipes and 24 "Fillings and Frostings!"

I closed the book and got ready to write a check. "How much?" I asked. "Sorry," the dealer said, "The White House Cook Book is sold." She saw that I was about to spill tears right there on the Fayette High School basketball floor. She hesitated a moment and added, "These two people just bought it for a Mother's Day gift." I turned, scowling—there stood my Nancy and Walt, grinning! 🐦

OLD GRAY MOUSE

As far as the tackle box is concerned, I'm a pack rat. I hurriedly paw through the clutter, especially when the sun is fading into dusk. That's when I expect the bass and bluegill to go wild for surface bugs in our backyard pond.

Just before sunset this evening, I stared into that tackle box full of memories. There was the bare cork, rough-whittled, with a too-big hook in it, which my dear old Dad made. This ugly, unpainted cork-and-hook concoction, which is held together with heavy black cotton mending thread, reminds me that Dad was a plain no-nonsense man who went after big, stupid, hungry fish. "Those crazy-looking lures attract fishermen, but they scare old country bass," he'd say.

My tackle box also hides the first plug I ever made. It's a pine stick that I whittled down to the size of my thumb. After sanding and painting it white, I added decal scales and eyes and put on two treble hooks and a nose ring. This glorified fugitive from the wood pile caught a keeper bass on my very first cast!

My fishing time is important as a private, quiet time to just enjoy being alive. What a Sunday! It started with a beautiful sunrise and a fresh morning walk. We heard a good sermon and had dinner at the cafeteria; no dishes to wash. Our adult children stopped by during the afternoon with our four grandsons. We had peanut butter for supper.

Scrounging through the tackle box, I discovered Old Gray Mouse, a deer hair thing I'd made during World War II. "Poor old mouse," I said aloud. "I should have tossed you out years ago."

I brushed his hair backwards to try to fluff him up to look alive. No luck! The hook was rusty, the deer hair stained brown. I looked at the thing and thought, "Your eyes have washed away through the years and your whiskers are completely gone. Poor Old Mouse."

But I was remembering my first big bass, a three and a half pounder, which I caught years ago in Ham Holt's little pond about three o'clock on a sultry summer afternoon—on this Old Gray Mouse.

"No fish would come out on a hot day like this," someone had said, but we went anyway. I sent Mouse to the far side of that little pond and he squatted down nicely under an overhanging willow limb. WHAM! My fly rod bent. I hadn't taken net or stringer because it was such an unlikely fishing day. I backed up into the pasture to drag him out of the water.

That Mouse had seen a lot of bass lips since then, but now he was a goner. Just for old time's sake, however, I tied him to my leader for one last cast. I placed him out under an overhanging willow, just as I had done that hot afternoon at Ham Holt's pond. I jiggled him a bit and waited, remembering when Mouse was born.

I had gone to New York City during World War II, traveling

on a Greyhound bus at 35 mph. It was a hard trip. Chub was in Diesel engine school and had a two-hour break each afternoon. One day I visited a craft shop and bought fly-tying materials "complete with instruction book." My first lures were woolly worms and black gnats on hooks of various sizes.

Oops! I was startled back to the present. Something actually struck at old mouse. I saw a flash of silver scales. Then the line went limp. Enjoying the memories, I left the old lure on the surface, tightening my line, just in case.

In that fly-tying kit there was a three-inch square of deer body hair. I learned how to wrap the waxed thread around a tuft of the hollow deer body hairs and how to make the hairs stand out in all directions. After adding more tufts of deer hair until the hook was almost covered, I snipped the hairs to the size and shape of a mouse. Mouse-making was fun. I kept that first one to remember those long hours of waiting in a cheap New York City hotel.

Wham! A nine-inch bluegill with a lot of dash and daring was mine. Old Mouse was still alive! Removing that rusty hook, I discovered a wad of loose, stained deer body hairs in the bluegill's mouth. The rusty hook was empty except for some of the thread. I loosened the leader knot with the flip of my thumbnail, cradled Old Gray Mouse in the hollow of my hand for a moment and said, "Thanks."

Then quickly, lest I back out, I clamped a sinker to the rusty hook, wrapped the remaining thread around the tuft of deer body hair and tossed Mouse into the deepest part of our farm pond. Forever!

No wonder it took seven years to say, "I do."

BEST FRIENDS FOR SIXTY-SEVEN YEARS

It was brazen of me—sending a comic valentine to a handsome ROTC soldier in wrinkled uniform. It was one of those ugly comics on rough paper, ridiculing the male college student. That was in 1931 and I was a high school junior; he was a student in the School of Engineering at the University of Missouri. We had smiled at each other a few times in the parking lot which was between University High School and the Engineering building.

Then on February 24th he wrote me a long note, ending with, "Why didn't you stop this morning? You'd have been as welcome as a rose in January." We began to eat our lunches in his old Pontiac truck in the parking lot. His depression job was to pick up cans of milk from ten farms and deliver them to dairies in Columbia.

As an ROTC student he marched in uniform on Wednesday afternoons on the campus near the columns. I used to watch the performance, getting an occasional glimpse of Walter Frank (Chub) Gerard with a riflery medal on his chest.

In December I was to read the Christmas Bible story at

Little Bonne Femme Baptist Church as children acted out the nativity scene. To make a favorable impression on my new friend, I stood tall and recited it without looking at the Bible in my hand. He liked that.

We attended Olivet Christian Church where I was a member and we also attended the Presbyterial Student Association where Chub and the other fellows prepared a 20-cent supper every Sunday evening. I paid for my own football and basketball tickets and for occasional movies. We were poor but so were our friends.

We joined a group of young married couples who had card parties, swimming trips, picnics and other inexpensive events. I played fiddle for square dances and Chub learned to dance. He'd drive me home in his worn out truck and I'd sometimes fall asleep with my head on his lap. Marriage wasn't mentioned. We both lived with our parents. By the time he was in his third year of engineering, I had entered the School of Journalism. We had saved our "cigarette money" to buy Chub some woodworking tools and he made beautiful things out of scraps of old walnut furniture. We also owned a dog together and a postal savings account. We were driving a little 1927 Chevy coupe that Chub had assembled from part of a truck plus a $25 body—our first car! In the fall of 1935 I was a senior in the School of Journalism and, surprisingly, was employed to teach ten hours of swimming each week at Christian College.

We traded the $25 Chevy coupe in on a big old Plymouth four-door sedan, sharing the cost. Chub was still hauling cans of milk to dairies and hauling the clean cans back to farms about five o'clock each afternoon.

We had been welcomed into each other's families during our

seven years of platonic friendship. In May of 1937, my Mother died following a sudden illness. All of us were crushed. Dad planned to quit the dairy business. As we discussed that possibility, it became obvious that he and Chub could form a partnership. Dad would lend us the money to buy into the dairy. He would continue to own the cows and sell milk to the partnership. We'd call it Meyers and Gerard Dairy. It was a good plan. Dad had renewed incentive, Chub had a job and we could marry and have the rest of our lives together as man and wife. We started the enterprise with a beautiful new white 1938 Dodge delivery truck and Chub was the delivery man.

On December 27, 1937, we were married in our living room with the Christmas decorations and gifts still displayed. We withdrew $35 from the bank to add to the pocket money we had on hand. Happy as larks, we headed for a wedding trip south in our '35 Plymouth sedan. We had a flat about eight miles from home and had to buy an inner tube at Ashland. Motels cost about $2.50 per night and we paid for one good meal a day. For breakfast we split a quart of milk and ate doughnuts and bananas. We arrived home on New Year's Eve with just a little pocket change to spare.

Thus began our 60 happy years together. We vowed that we'd never be too poor to travel. Chub said, "I'll make the living and you can make the travel money." In five years we were almost out of debt, but dairy supplies were hard to get. Tires, stainless steel and other essential materials had gone to the war effort. Chub decided that he should go to war too. He enlisted in the U.S. Coast Guard and served three years.

We sold the retail dairy but Dad kept the cows and sold wholesale milk to the bigger dairies. I stayed on at Christian

College where my salary crept up a little every year.

Our children were born after the war; Nancy in 1949 and Walt in 1951. Walt was two when we bought our 160-acre farm for $4500. It was cut up with gullies and overgrown by weeds and sprouts, but Dad helped us terrace and fertilize it. We named it Whip-Poor-Will Hill because we loved the night call of those unusual birds.

After the war Chub worked as assistant manager of the local Rural Electric Co-op (REA) and I stayed on at Christian until 1972 (with four years out when the babies were young). When Nancy and Walt were six and four, we built a simple little swimming pool in the backyard. More and more people enrolled for lessons so we enlarged it to 45' x 15' and I taught classes for two months each summer. The kids helped me and Nancy eventually took over on her own. True to our vow to travel, we made numerous family camping trips together.

The years flew by too fast and soon Nancy and Walt had homes of their own. Our lives were enriched by the births of Sam Russell and Cole Gerard in 1979, Peter Gerard in 1980, and Oliver Gerard in 1982. For several summers I had our grandchildren here on Whip-Poor-Will Hill for "Granny's Day Camp".

Suddenly our kids and their kids are grown and I'm 84 years old! I'm in good health, swimming 300 yards almost every day this summer in the backyard pool. I'm expecting to get my hands in the clay again very soon. But now I'm going it alone. Chub died at age 88, two months after we celebrated our 60 years of married life.

I couldn't ask for our lives to have been any better.

PHOTO CREDITS

Thanks to the many photographers (known and unknown) who have contributed to this book.

Connie Baskett, 8 center (top left)

Alan Borrud, 270

Dr. Lewis Garrotto, 170

Sue Gerard, 71, 78, 128, 135, 136, 140, 152, 156, 164, 179, 195, 198, 204, 209, 214, 248, 254, 263 (left), 1 center (bottom left), 2 center, 3 center (bottom right), 4 center (bottom left), 5 center (top right), 6 center, 8 center (top right and bottom left)

William Helvey, 7 center

Walt Johnson-Gerard, 5 center (top left and bottom)

Jeff Joiner, 4 center (bottom right)

Mid Lytle, 1 center (bottom right)

J.D. Meyers, 60 (photo of painting)

Nancy Henry Meyers, 106

Marion Pease, 111

Cheryl Riley, dedication picture

Lyle Schertz, 233

Smith Studios, 115